Love's Seasons

D1736318

Reviews

Journey with Kathryn as she shares with you her immersion in nature, her love of family, her global trotting and her meditation on love. These poems are honest, and as infinite as the myriad faces of nature. The lines whisper like petals unfurling, and by the end of the poems, the brilliant blooms are evident. *Love's Seasons* is a bouquet you will want to keep for yourself, but also happy to share.

Opal Palmer Adisa, Author of *4-Headed Woman*, Professor, Writer

In *Love's Seasons*, Kathryn Takara has captured the complexities of feminine essence. Clearly she has listened to her heart, the hearts of other women, and the female heartthrobs in nature. Kathryn has delivered these expressions through relatable passages. The appeal is gender universal as women can identify with the in-depth, multi-dimensional reflections; and men have the opportunity to learn about the wonderful intricacies of femininity.

Bonnyeclaire Smith-Stewart, CEO and Founder, 4 Million Voices, Inc.

Takara continues to produce for us poems that are personal, romantic, spicy, funny, and inspiring. *Love's Seasons* consists of fresh, new, and collected poems touching part of our senses that often need special stimulation. In these poems, Takara acknowledges her African, Native American, and European ancestries that are the roots of her being. Because she is a sensitive woman, her Hawaiian experiences have helped guide her on her chosen path of creativity. We thank her for this gift.

Miles M. Jackson, Professor Emeritus, University of Hawai`i at Mānoa

Between Alabama and Ka`a`awa there is a vast ocean of consciousness composed of a movement of infinitesimal water particles in a perfect and perennial dance with the infinitude of life forms. Dr. Waddell Takara captures the mystery of life and beyond with her precise cadence in sync with the divine love constantly generated by the vast and infinitesimal movement. Her open-ended poetics of sensuality transforms the "I" into an effect, inviting readers to experience at first hand the process of becoming-nature, becoming-cosmos, and becoming-whole on a molecular level of existence.

Masahide T. Kato, Assistant Professor, University of Hawai`i at West O`ahu

OTHER BOOKS BY THIS AUTHOR

Timmy Turtle Teaches. Children's book. Ka`a`awa, HI: Pacific Raven Press, 2012.

Frank Marshall Davis: The Fire and the Phoenix (A Critical Biography). Ka`a`awa, HI: Pacific Raven Press, 2012.

Tourmalines: Beyond the Ebony Portal. Ka`a`awa, HI: Pacific Raven Press, 2010.

*Pacific Raven: Hawai`i Poems*. Ka`a`awa, HI: Pacific Raven Press, 2009. (Winner of 2010 American Book Award from the Before Columbus Foundation.)

New and Collected Poems. Berkeley, CA: Ishmael Reed Publishing, 2003.

Oral Histories of African Americans. Interviews by Kathryn Waddell Takara. Center for Oral History. Social Science Research Institute. Honolūlū, HI: University of Hawai`i at Mānoa, 1990.

CREDITS

"The Advancing Day Reveals" ["Contemplation"]. *The Bamboo Muse: Art, Prose, Poetry*. By Alonzo Davis et al. Edited by Kay S. Lindsey. 2010.

"Patchouli Burning." ["Patchouli. "] Editor's Award. International Society of Poets. Spring 2004.

"Cantos of Love." ["Cantos."] *The Voice*. Honorable Mention. Poetry Contest for Building Fund. National Association of Letter Carriers. March 1996.

"Bird's View." *Hawai`i Review 20* Fall 1986.

"Payment." *Hawai`i Review 19* Spring 1986.

LOVE'S SEASONS
Generations Genetics Myths

Kathryn Waddell Takara

Edited by Mera Moore

Pacific Raven Press

Ka`a`awa, Hawai`i
http://pacificravenpress.co/

Pacific Raven Press LLC
Ka`a`awa, Hawai`i 96730

ISBN: 9 780986 075506

Catalogued as: Poetry, African American, History, Memoir

Library of Congress Cataloging-in-publication data
Love's Seasons: Generations, Genetics, Myths by Kathryn Waddell Takara,
PhD

Book Cover and Layout Design by Jonathan Zane, Eien Design Studio LLC

This work is licensed under Pacific Raven Press LLC.
Printed in the United States of America

Pacific Raven Press, LLC, is an independent publisher.
http://pacificravenpress.co/

DEDICATION

To Lottie Y and Apple
(my parents)

TABLE OF CONTENTS

III. DARKENED ROOMS: Spicy Rides

ACKNOWLEDGEMENTS

This book is a rite of passage into a courageous speaking-out period of my life. It is a time of serving and knowing, a time of reckoning and accepting, even a time of talking back. All of this on the subject of love.

There are many people to acknowledge and thank, you who have offered me encouragement, support, and various gifts to assist me in developing my being, writing, and speaking—studying and guiding me to this phase of my living and practice. This is our accomplishment.

I offer sincere and joyful gratitude to the Divine Source of endless energy and creativity for providing me light, in the forms of knowledge, people, family, animals, and the environment, enabling me to see if sometimes only fleetingly the various dimensions and expressions of love. To listen and hear the sounds from the unseen realms of reality, to sense and respect the rich cultural traditions of my many and varied ancestors, to travel, experience, and earn understanding, and to be available to the ever-changing conditions and opportunities of the moment are priceless gifts.

There are my cherished earth family and friends, especially those creative souls, thinkers, philosophers, psychologists, writers and editors such as Ishmael Reed, Mera Moore, Paul Lyons, Karla Brundage, Katherine Orr, and Allison Francis; musicians from Bach and Kalapana to Stevie Wonder and Aretha; poets including Rumi, Hafiz, and Mary Oliver; artists, leaders, and teachers like Keskenan, Streetz, XJ Kennedy, Mathieson, Henningsen, Cahill, and Manicas; my mentors and innumerable eager students; and all who generously and repeatedly shared their time, values, principles, practices, and feedback, food, wine, talents, dance, rituals, inspiration, and love.

There are those who encouraged me to travel within myself and out into the world, who taught me how to see colors and light, to feel the vibrations of people and nature. They taught me how to research, observe, dissect, analyze, and simply stop and listen, to hear the voices of music and life itself.

Some just let me sit and be, offered their space, shared special places, while others offered words of encouragement and endless readings of my writing and manuscripts as I morphed and grew through the decades. Others helped me heal the body, mind, soul, and spirit, offered and shared tools to change old patterns and transform to better ways of thinking, emptying, being, meditation and stillness, the laying on of hands, visualization, songs and chants, dance, taiji and qigong, books, and affirmations to lift me up when I became discouraged.

To each and all of you, I offer my deep gratitude and humbly bow.

FOREWORD

Women are shape shifters in the cloudy winds
of communication
compassion subverted by irregular character
buffeted by unpredictable excursions emotional.
Diaphanous revelations arrive on a clearing
high up along the perilous path to transformation.
Consolation flies by: healing and pleasure within view.

Love's Seasons follows the threads of generations and processes: inheritance and family, the myth and reality of romantic love, the earthbound materialism of its nurturing magic, the losing and recovering of personal identity, the service and surrender to love's healing, and the transcendence of the individual's integrity, sacrifice, and suffering to the service of a higher good. I celebrate the rituals of initiation, courtship, marriage, birth, and death. There is the wildness and willfulness of youth, the struggle to take control of the self and the heart in the middle years, and the learning to ask and listen—to relate and make correspondences—in maturity. Overall, the book addresses regeneration and mystical transformation.

Women are shape shifters—assuming many forms, playing many roles—culture bearers, teachers, and seekers of life and divinity. Women are resourceful, brave warriors because of subtly hostile powers of hidden dominance that cross their paths and hinder their progress. Women are instinctive survivors for posterity and the children that they bring forth and nurture for success. Women are healing agents who use common sense, intuition, beauty, alchemy, and bright inspiration to walk through challenging experiences. Women are the stuff mythology is made of. Women are communicators, effusive yet concise. Their responsibility is to balance emotion and reason, procreate, serve freely, heal, learn the dances and stories of the ancestors, and bear witness. In this place where I write, sometimes my spirit sings, sensing a slight hint of summer breeze, a taste of watermelon fresh. I follow up the ladder of the wise ones, write brightly, voicing myths birthed in fears, tears, forgiveness, and transformation. I honor the ancestors as spirit guides, our protectors. I celebrate the oral tradition and the spoken word, so valuable to those old souls who are awake and eager to listen and learn, who treasure the love of family and friends. I offer these poems of inner explorations that reflect both dead ends and openings.

Through the poems in this book, the reader goes on a rhythmic journey into the deep world of love, where Nature is resplendent and secretive, a metaphor of the feminine. Other common metaphors are the winds, waters, moon, stars, sun, seasons, planting, weeding, and harvesting. The fierce power and magic of love and its mysteries, the intensity of passion, and the longing of absence are predominant themes in this collection. The subjects include family, friends, lovers, sensuality, loss, and letting go.

"Our first teacher is our heart" is a Cheyenne saying. My known ancestry is African, Cherokee, French, German, English, Irish, Scottish, and Welsh. What stories have I to tell in these poems? I feel the breath of our ancestors. I listen to and record ancestral voices in the spirits of earth, water, wind, and fire, as well as living voices of people in my everyday life.

Poetry is a healing language of the heart and emotions. The poet skillfully uses metaphors coupled with the masterful intellect to produce correspondences for the reader. I agree with the Kikuyu saying, "Earth is the mother of all that is life." The creative process heals and transforms. Witness the birth of precious feelings, boundless love, deep happiness, pure pleasure, harmony, and the unlimited expectancy of the good.

The iwa bird soars above, over, and beyond the trees and contours of the visible. The banyan puts out many roots from above and transcends the ordinary correspondences to make connections between heaven and earth. The poet smiles and illuminates new ways of perception, flying high and observing, foreshadowing the healing rains. There is the intense realization and experience that helps one to forgive. Often, joyful imagination and conscience guide our feet along the karmic path to wisdom.

~Kathryn Waddell Takara, Ph.D., July 2014

INTRODUCTION

Growing Together:
Introduction to Kathryn Waddell Takara's Love's Seasons

By Paul Lyons, Ph.D., University of Hawai`i at Mānoa

As I open this volume of loving and generous poems I imagine the lights glowing blue, and Kathryn Takara stepping to a microphone, frangipani behind her ear, to fill the room with the calls and cadences of her voice. This is to say that an intimate, conversational, spoken quality infuses the poems—we are invited to overhear them as secondary lovers: "Come and walk with me/in the forest of poetry," Takara writes in "Room for You," "where the message of moonlight/is written on the leaves." The attendant reader will be gifted by her frank lyricism, her amplitude in sharing ecstatic, sensuous, or bandaged moments of the heart.

From the opening sequence—on bloodlines, Tuskegee, and her parents Lottie Y and Apple—Love's Seasons approaches her poetic journey as an elaboration of relationships. The first order of relation, genealogical, begins by valuing what has been and is to be bequeathed across the generations, in particular by steadfast and brave women. (We learn that her mother, an avid reader of historical novels, named the poet after Katherine the Great.) Takara witnesses her own story shaped by her parents' creativity and refusals of Jim Crow exclusions. Her life is the fruit of their choices, as stories for her children grow in the belly of the life she leads.

The poems thereby celebrate the "family ladder/rungs leading to the heart," the joining of legacies into "rhythms of family/As true and reliable/As the towering mountains of these islands" ("Celebrating Marriage"). Significantly, the phrase "these islands" wants no referent in this collection, as the Hawaiian archipelago has become central in Takara's life, rich soil on which her daughters have been born, living ground that nourishes her spirit.

The solidity of ancestry and the materiality of family history anchor the collection, and echo forward through Takara's descriptions of love's seasons. These are described in individual sections, in which the poet by turns basks and soars in the rhapsodic, unmediated light of The Beloved; romps through "spicy rides"; sashays through erotic and turquoise moods; weathers seas of harsh absence, ache, separation and loss; grows resilient recalling love in far places; and all the while accommodates desire to the changing world.

The poet's movements across physical space—her childhood in Ala-
bama; her settling in Ka'a'a'wa, in country O'ahu; her travels to rap-
idly developing Beijing—have their correlatives in aesthetic and philo-
sophical transformations, as well as in the passions of body and spirit.

In Takara's lines, desire joins with its object. That her beach-walk matter-
of-fact perceptions of "a light/brighter than love/that scarred my heart/
vaster than the ocean/that glowed in the night" ("Brighter Than Venus in
Honolūlū") echo across the centuries with the metaphysical poet Henry
Vaughan's "I saw Eternity the other night,/Like a great ring of pure and end-
less light,/All calm, as it was bright" presents as a kind of proof. Anticipa-
tion itself is charged when the Beloved remains absent or placed in question:

> Your presence runs like music
> from sky to sky of my being
>
> But you are hidden
> like the moon behind the cloud. ("My Song")

For the believing-loving heart, that we miss the numinous from a clouded
position does not mean that the light isn't there. Afterglow too heats the
skin: "Until I see you again," writes the poet in "Waiting for Daybreak,"
"only the great ocean can cool me." In fact, the direct address of many of
the poems, echoing Rumi and the Songs of Solomon, argues the centrality
of responsiveness: "woman knocks, love's door opens." Takara enacts the
joys of educating one's own wild heart to swing "open to intuitive messages/
and new doors" ("Walk Strong"). In that service, as she writes in "Blood-
lines," the poems "witness, marvel, and write"—"marvel" as in an active
receptiveness to the available-marvelous that is thrown together in every-
day life, and that runs counter to greed-driven and terracidal perception.

Within a desire that draws energy to tell itself from many great wisdom tradi-
tions of the world, and a harvest of personal experience, divinity dances in
the details. The poems cherish small, found moments: smells of baking and
holiday wreathes in an expecting kitchen ("Waiting for Baby"); the imprints
a saxophone makes on an impressionable heart ("Your Sax"); findings among
shoreline debris of green balls of sea-smoothed glass ("Gathering Glass").

Though such discoveries love streams across time and place into a rich
garden of the heart. Takara plants and works here; fragrant lehua, puak-
enikeni, and night-blooming pikake blossom alongside the lotus; trea-
sured crystals throw colors over a koa wood table: it is a cultivated, de-
voted space, where people, ideas, and poems may grow together.

Love's Seasons

SHAPE SHIFTERS

Ledges and Ladders

BLOODLINES

I marvel at generations of bloodlines
genetics apparent in the curve of a chin
the lilt of a head, the smile or laugh
resemblances in body language
the texture of the hair, the shape of the buttocks
the curve of the calf, the height, the girth, the voice.

Perceived qualities of inaccurate memory
marvelously become strong men and beautiful women.

Family lines are cracked-open windows
to reveal Nature's serendipitous similarities
the balance and miracles of family.

To study our ancestry is to expand our horizon of self
to witness the patterns, struggles, and successes of being
including love's vagrant and influential seasons.

I witness, marvel, and write.

TUSKEGEE

Tuskegee
divine mirror of to-do attitudes
black folk, hard work, rewards of success
diamond of a small southern town
    mined from dark slavery, sharecropping, miscegenation, and born
    in dreams.

Students walked miles to arrive
        with one change of clothes and determination
        to labor, to learn, to progress themselves and the race
        to seek an education, help to build a school, a campus
Students made the bricks one by one, cultivated the grounds
        and built the Tuskegee Institute Chapel in 1898
            renowned towering stained-glass windows
            precious colors, royal gems.

A whole community witnessed the great midnight fire
        destruction of the *bellisimo* cathedral chapel in 1957
        flames seen from my house 2-1/2 miles away
        knew fear, understood endings
        listened to rumors of KKK violence
remembered burning crosses, vulnerable churches.

Tuskegee
        people watched the recurring tragedies of race
           so connected yet disconnected
           by color and class and unknown quilted histories
           whispered in closets, behind doors, in bedrooms
Where the brotherly love?

Trepidations of whites dominated the unspoken discourse
        fears of educated articulate uppity niggahs
           who sang Jubilee songs and spirituals, traveled, and got
           degrees.

Blacks thrived, got jobs, created jobs, researched and learned black history
    understood the value of black pride and self help.

Chief Anderson, light-skinned and confident
        taught the Tuskegee Air Men at Moton Field
        took up Eleanor Roosevelt in his plane—she dared fly with a black
        man!

My Dad, Bill Waddell, walnut brown and handsome
        came to Tuskegee to work on peanut-oil therapy with George
        Washington Carver
        to research a liniment for those paralyzed by polio
        like President Roosevelt who reluctantly visited the campus with
        his wife.

My Mom, Lottie, proud, smart as a whip, fabulously stylish
        from a well-to-do family who owned land and had servants
        descended from generations of teachers, she taught languages
        even after marriage, when women were expected to stay home she
        kept her job.

I see so many mind pictures
family resemblances, processes evolving.

Tuskegee, prototype of hard work and determination so much history,
        open and hidden.

WHEN I WAS A CHILD

The mythology of me
a good child, obedient, "Yes Ma'am"
sweet as sugar
"Can I help you, Mama?"
in the security of a comfortable home
a college town in a deep southern state
surrounded by pine forests, cotton fields, dirt-poor people, and Jim Crow.

Growing up, I loved to get up early
eat a big breakfast on the tall kitchen table
with Daddy, who was always cooking something good
for me, his "Miss Sweetnin"
fried apples, thick rind bacon
and sometimes he'd cut
one of the several 2-foot-long watermelons
resting in rows on the back porch and sitting on each step
fruit he got from cash strapped farmers as payment for his veterinary services.

Today
I dwell far away in a place of rich soil among tolerant people
the island surroundings tropical, colorful, almost harmonious
leaves new and plump like childhood
undamaged greens, buds, flowers
emerging fruits nurtured by Nature's breakfast: showers, sun, and rainbows.

ASIAN REFLECTIONS OF A BLACK WOMAN

Wo ai ni = "I love you," in Mandarin

In a dream when I was ten years old
landlocked and racially marginalized
I saw a pearl of a city
surrounded by the sea
while I was contained in a land of pine.

Wo ai ni, cha cha chu
Wo ai ni, cha cha chu.

Trees were all around
tall as the sky
taller than emotions
when I feared bullwhip snakes
and the hateful county sheriff.

Stars were bright as diamonds
in night's canopy of unknown
currents of hatred and fears
eddied around like the water moccasins
down by the creek near the Air Base
where the Tuskegee pilots practiced, became tough experts
buzzed the houses of friends
under the mindful guidance of Chief Anderson.

Wo ai ni, cha cha chu
Wo ai ni, cha cha chu.

But who was I
excluded from trying on hats, shoes, clothes
excluded from public movie theaters and the local swimming pool
excluded from libraries and segregated city facilities
blood quantum the hidden quicksand of a healthy ego?

Who was I
beyond the censored color of my skin?
Why was I
excluded from beaches, schools, restaurants, hotels?
What was the handicap
that circumscribed my possibilities?
Where was a road out
beyond the thundering tornadoes and lightning of discrimination?

Could would should I not accept my alleged inferior status
the lynching of African identity
in extremes of southern emotions?
Fiery pain smoldered in antiquated paradigms
rage jazzed in discordant tones of Stravinsky and Adderly.

What did I want, need to grow?
How were my waters poisoned
my confidence eroded by alien authority
hostile blockages and stereotypes
unequal economics and enforced ignorance?
When did the negative self-construction begin
and grow to a river of impotence?
I struggled in raging currents of self doubt
in the rudderless boats of eddying black history
Always questions camouflaged just below articulation
How to overcome the fear of failure?
How to break the barrier of imposed superiority and take risks?

If I could but discover the pearl of freedom
rebellious wishes and dreams of a young black girl
whose being was navigated by the privilege of whiteness
whose unarticulated longings
were nurtured by faith, family, and legends of heroes
I was protected by the community
abundantly full of love and creativity
for its children and posterity, the stars of a new generation.

Wo ai ni, cha cha chu
Wo ai ni, cha cha chu.

I was a black pearl growing
in world travel and education
I discovered my freedom in the waters of knowledge
allowed myself to be found far from home
my shell broken open
my gifts of compassion, forgiveness freely given
writing became my wealth.

Wo ai ni, cha cha chu
Wo ai ni, cha cha chu.

PALE YELLOW

What I first remember
Was 2 years old or younger?
Waking up in my wooden crib
my bedroom, the middle one
painted pale yellow, flooded with early morning sunlight
sounds of birds wings fluttering in nearby bushes
sparrows tweeting, mockingbirds scolding, bluebirds chirping
smells familiar: morning dew heavy sweet air
honeysuckle shrubs, dogwoods
pink buds, pecan trees, pines
and Mama's high-yellow skin, smooth and soft.

What I first remember
standing shakily, holding the rail tightly
calling for Mama or Daddy to come
waiting to be picked up tenderly, taken out
have my cloth diaper changed
warm and heavy with pee pee
waiting looking out my 2 tall windows
over the crepe myrtle
across the glowing green lawn
beyond the perfectly trimmed hedge
to the pine forest.

What I first remember
listening for familiar footsteps in the hall
from Mama's room, the bathroom, or the kitchen
her voice reassuring, saying, "I'm coming, Kay,"
her loving smile appearing around the door
happy to see me, hold me, take care of me.

I remember and am comforted by this memory
of luminous yellow love.

WHO WAS MY MAMA?

What Mama said
Mama did.
"Be the words."
She smelled good
Ponds and *Toujours Moi*
Lingering Camel cigarette smoke.

She wore her fabulous and abundant wardrobe
sharp suits and dresses bought from Bonwit Teller in New York City
French perfume, hats, and gloves
AAA high-heeled shoes
along with pricey gifts of jewelry from my Dad.

She drove Buicks exclusively
for almost 50 years
loved to play tennis and throw parties
played serious bridge with Lionel Richie's mom
enjoyed canasta with Booker T. Washington's granddaughter.

She worked hard and had "help"
housekeepers, cooks, and others who weekly washed and ironed
scrubbed and babysat when I was small and underfoot.
She entertained sometimes hosting catered events
taught me to make petit-four sandwiches
and "to serve properly, if you please."

Mama always had students live with us
in exchange for tuition, room and board
young men who did yard work and handyman chores
young women who knew how to bake from scratch
sew beautiful dresses, and do lovely embroidery.

Mama was a professor of 3 languages
French, German, English with 2 MA degrees.
She was a Delta, a thespian, a dedicated wife and mother.
She played the piano well, but could not carry a good tune.
Still she sang to me daily when she practiced on the Steinway.
Mamma was a good sister, cousin, niece, and loyal friend
miserable with migraines, intelligent with books, and fun in an intimate group.

Mama enjoyed historical novels
naming me after Katherine the Great of Russia
but she spelled it differently: Kathryn.
She was agnostic, refused to gossip
had a warm heart and a cool demeanor among strangers.
She hated segregation and inferior status
challenged Jim Crow laws when we traveled
making me embarrassed and afraid.

Mama was full of contradictions, brave yet shy
popular yet lonely, proud yet insecure.
I would learn that her parents died young, and her mother was murdered.
Orphaned at 8, she lived with family until she married.
Mama was lucky and loved by many, especially her husband.
No second-class citizen would she ever be!
She was always the lady.

CELEBRATING MARRIAGE

Dance a memory of seasons, holidays
Together bonding with
Something greater
Yin Yang
Different yet connected
Family ladder
Rungs leading to the heart.

Big surf surprises
Heavy rains drench the earth
The blues slide in with the mud and gloom.
Sun follows, shines
Surreptitiously strong
On each in our family
Nature's songs resonate
Felt by all
Perceived individually.

Drums vibrate collectively
The heartbeat the hope of the marriage
A transcendent connector of the planet
Passed on like cultures
Love courses mythical
The legacy of the clan
A genetic effecter of history.

Vision of time passing
An illusion
Babies transforming to adults and elders
Whales appearing in winter then disappearing in late spring
As real and unreal as permanence.

Puffy clouds float by
Seasonal storms pound
Then all is clear again
Family continues, grows, something greater spawns a legacy.
Together we seek calm
We gather again for the rituals
At our home of dreams
Legacy of the ancestors' knowing.

We two remember
Float on the hanging chairs
In the perfumed garden
Under sweet mangos of presence
Grown from seeds in the compost
Brought here 30 years ago from your boyhood home.

We continue sometimes blindly along
At times unseeing unfeeling even unreliable
Forgetting the moments
The mystery and magic of family connections and special vows.

The persistent movement of energy
Through births, struggles, and enduring links
Supports understanding
Seasons of family
Together and apart
Budding, blooming, falling
From Father Sky
To Mother Earth and Sister Sea
Rhythms of connections, correspondences, commitments
True and reliable as acceptance and forgiveness
As the towering mountains of these islands.

HEAVENLY CIRCLES

Children are our flowers
seeds of love come human
a heartbeat extended like holy beads
a chant
OM . . .
HU . . .

We bring the babies to our mothers
our fathers, our families
we as water for each other
breathing, thinking, feeling
familiar . . . growing.

Later
they fall from our trees
we feel barren, less beautiful
remotely comforted with the thought
that they grow strong on the edge of our cliffs
that we have given them guidance and hope.

Our children in turn will have children
whom we wish more harmony and understanding
than we had and shared with our own.

We toast to their growth, their efforts, their successes
spiraling upward like blossoms on a bright breeze
that they too may provide a heavenly dance
of healing and knowledge to those who follow
gratitude for those too old to cross another generation
and seek only a peaceful place from which to rest and watch
the parade of generations.

AUTUMN GIFT

The full harvest moon announces November
orange as Halloween crepe paper
I wrap your birthday presents
and write a little note.
Here I am
thinking of you
packing sweets, nuts, fragrances
rocks from a visit to Yellowstone
shells from the nearby North Shore
colorful clips to tame your hair
crunches of crisps from Maui.
I reminisce full of love
Smell sweet jasmine and *pikake*
imagine *Kwan Yin* bathed moonlight
beside a clear pool
full of lotus flowers.
I tie bright copper and ginger colored ribbons
to transport to you with this fall package.

WAITING FOR BABY

It was a cold day in Oakland
Cold, wet, and welcome
After the New Year celebration and waiting
The narcissus and daffodils opening expectantly
Even as red and yellow leaves still falling
Down to the winter's welcoming earth.

The house was warm and cozy with Tati's baking
Mac cheese, roast chicken, and homemade applesauce
Still the baby did not come.

The last day of the winter's solstice
Mama was ready to take care of her
Daddy was at Mama's side
Music played in the sun room
Strewn with brother's trucks and trains galore.

This night in the season of Capricorn
The moon will mark the twelfth day of Christmas
The magic of Epiphany
The sun will start to set later
The days will get brighter.

It was a cold day in December
The second decade of a new century
Daddy and Mama decided to go out for pizza
Since the child was not yet ready to leave the warm womb
Not ready to be born into the waiting family
While near and far family and friends anticipated another new beginning.

WELCOME POEM

Dear sweet child whom I have yet to meet
You came to us in January
A Capricorn child like me, your grandmother, Tati
A granddaughter after my heart and planetary energies.
We, the family, welcome you and celebrate your coming
Even though you were late and troublesome in the process
Almost 10 pounds, imagine!
Now, newly named Mia.

Jubilant and joy-filled at your presence
New and old tribes, ancestors, and we your family all rejoice.
Dear beautiful child
You were determined and fierce on arrival
Insisting on milk before it came in.
You had to wait impatiently
Like we waited for you.

Now you rest peacefully in your tired Mama's arms
Who smiles and holds you warm and close.
Your daddy, sister, and brother embrace you tenderly
Supporting each other and your beloved mother
Excited to get to know you and for you to know them.
When will I meet you, precious child?

PINK

Pink a color for girls,
frilly, lacy, easily soiled.

Pink baby blanket, bubble gum, jacket,
beach towel hanging behind the bathroom door.

Pink ribbons and barrettes
for braids and Sunday curls.

Pink Easter eggs, organdy dresses,
pink ruffled socks and bonnets.

Pink, a color of soft youth,
suggesting security, not strife.

Pink, the color of dogwood blossoms
in March on the side of our house.

Pink the color of the bathroom tiles
in the Alabama home where I grew up.

Pink, a color of sunset or sunrise,
pillowed between oranges, reds, blues, and purples.

Pink is for roses, tropical ginger flowers, exotic drinks,
wedding petals, vacations, and satin seductions.

Pink is for effeminate moments,
like bubbling cold champagne after orgasms.

Electric pinks on tight shorts worn by punkers, joggers, bikers, and roller-
bladers
and on chartreuse *pareo* wraps, worn by hula dancers.

Pink is for cotton candy, grey slacks, and pink shirts,
pink houses and Cadillacs punctuating subdivisions in Florida.

Pink is for the dreamtime, visitations of swans,
Cheshire cats, dragonflies, and magic rides on soap-bubble carpets.

WOMAN'S WORK

Bearer of tradition
in a field of foreign
she remembers the ancients
nurturing moments in performance
exercising her wings of New Age
Aquarian gatherer.

She who remembers
the dance to the center
the harmony of humming
She drums the red rhythms of moon rituals
on her thighs, chants invocations to the angel of joy.

She is the dream carrier
but not the dream
mother and earth incomplete.

Illness of overwork swoops down in a lunge
sudden like stumbling energy dislocation
light shatters in shards of sick.

She falls in a ball
rests like a gourd
rolls on the winter ground
gathering her smoldering powers.

She returns secretly
to the sacred green place within
lights a fire at her hidden altar
awaiting the Beloved
to balance her truth
to plant a vision
to share new seeds.
She awaits the appearance
the cleansing touch,
a healing breath of moment's love
transforming the fire to rain.

MOON RITUALS

Woman collecting flowers
Planting seeds
For a creative service in now
Harvesting herbs and beauty, perennial moon rituals.

Woman walking going
To the sacred pool
Gathering water in the gourd
Harboring a thirst for knowing.

Francophone woman drinks water
Feels pains of unrequited love.
She seizes air, moans
"Le Coeur m'en seigne"
You make my heart bleed.

Let go,
Le Coeur s'en seigne
He makes her heart bleed.
Elle saigne á la lanterne Parisienne
Whispers, "No more blood."

Sagace, the woman
Shrewd and secretive.
Elle cherche la sagesse,
she seeks wisdom in freedom
Elle voyage.

She *apparaît* at the *côte de Chine*
Gushes at the coast of ardent
Lights *saillit* like fireworks,
Burning passion born anew.
She prays for clear bubbling love
Dances breath
Knows the power of now.

Woman pauses at a new threshold
Le Côte d'Ivoire
Observes steadily
Acts, reacts, speaks
Discreet her words
"No longer can you make my heart bleed."

Woman knocks, love's door opens
She heats at a loving touch
Ripples fertile
Hot and wet between the legs
She flashes, leaps, bounds.

Woman slows down
Looks and learns
Inner kings and queens consort
Hopes and fears meet to balance
She climbs up steep ledge of crystal courage.

She envisions balance
Strong rock
Stable footing
Bright path and shimmering guide enhanced.
She finds protection in trust
Journeys up and around experience of the still mountains
Woman grows with new discovery of ladders and levels.

Woman appreciates
Looks for the best in others
Endures betrayal, accepts suffering
Deep within her core.

Woman nurtures, brings peace
To the digested corners of life
Respects organic growth and patterns of lunar creation.

Woman laughs with children

Blows up a red balloon, ties off and sings
Dances in circles around the trees
Runs in the wind with a kite
Conceives and births a clear space
Fresh rhythms feed growth and knowing.

Woman strobes radiant
Ever in search of the miraculous
Walks the pebbled path
Strewn with light and love.
Woman trips, stumbles, returns on her knees once again
To find an empty page
Picks up her favorite pen.

Woman writes, moon rituals birth understanding
Woman smiles, whispers serendipitous words of experience.
"Only she can make her own heart bleed."
Woman finally sleeps, fearless and free.

MAGNETISM

I sat in a pavilion on the China coast facing East
right after the World Cup Finals
with 3 friends, but you were not there.
After early morning *taiji*
meditation and prayers.
we reflected on the aspects of the mind:
perception, creativity, reasoning, memory.

I drifted in a daydream while they spoke
soared to astral.
My soul left my body
through my 3rd eye
unfolding through a fiery lotus meditation
not yet finished.

My being in suspended flight
sparkled and twinkled
across the international date line
on a magic carpet of miracle
threaded with aspects of golds and reds
peacock blues and greens
toward an island of the possible.
I soared in shimmering blue light
outside of time
to join you there.

I found myself next to you
on a beach in *Ka`a`awa*
in the middle of the Pacific
I felt the coconut breeze
on my bare brown skin
my friends unaware that my attention had left them.

Sparkling in your yellow space
I sat by your side again
on the familiar seacoast
far from the ancient land of jade
remembering how we laughed
selfishly kept our hands to ourselves
afraid to play like Lao Tzu

confinement Confucian
discipline practical.

But at this time of imagination
I touched you
insistently, heedlessly sighing
you could not ignore my invisible energy
I would not stop.

You were wide-eyed with wonder
not believing my presence
in your space.
"I saw you off on the plane,"
said your scientific voice.

For a few moments I sparkled
within your aura
a pink *pareo* on my narrow hips
a flower in my untamed hair.

You felt me, touched me
smelled my perfume
knew without question
I'd been with you
even in a dream.

Suddenly
I was in the pavilion again with my friends
no longer with you
happy to experience the power and wonder
a magical meditation in motion magnetic
feeling electric
feeling as one.

WALK STRONG

We women
genetic shape shifters in the cosmic wind
side step toward horn of the moon:
cloudy communication comes
through an open window in a lower room
crazy connections
confused by irregular character of being.

We women
buffeted by unpredictable excursions emotional
walk tall, remain hopeful and strong
open to intuitive messages
and new doors.

Revelations arrive on a bright clearing field
along the path to clarity:
we women excavate, explicate, extricate feeling
discover healing touch and pleasurable sensations
along the petal-strewn path toward transition.

We women are compassion
hard seeds, fragile blossoms, miracles of spring
open to challenging views.

We women, shape shifters
share alchemy of nurturing visions and voices
ride the invisible forces
beyond the clouds of limitation to experiences and places diverse

THE LIGHT OF YOU

Altered States

INTERIOR WILDERNESS

I.

The heart seduced
entangled by sparkling tendrils
alluring undergrowth.

The heart
wanting
waiting to be loved
unconditionally
waiting
fearing
imaginary beasts
dreading
pain --
the terrors
of boredom.
The heart
wanting to flee
yet charmed by love
needing acceptance
seeking comfort
in a tower of pleasure.

But is it love
that winks like a temptress
luring the unconscious heart
here and there
into the strangling twines
of emotion primal and ancient?

II.

How to escape
the snares of the heart?

Or does one tame this restless wilderness
like chopping vegetables
rendering all
into manageable pieces?

Love
strokes and pounds the heart
like leavening bread
until
perhaps
the heart walks hand in hand with her
like an old friend
serendipitous memories
after seasons of sufferings and healings
by the sun, moon, stars of persistence.

The heart
perennial sustenance of divine love
pushes forth and creates hopes
which break through the muddy wilderness
and tangled emotions.

A lotus opens in the dawn light
reaching for the intimate sky of harmony.

SPICY PROPOSAL

I expect to be hearing from you
despite estrangement, foreign relations
and Mercury in retrograde.
We are in that transcendent category
n'est-ce pas?

I You
in each other's dreams
two independent souls
sensing partnership
discovering breaths and being
harkening the ocean break
outside of time's essence.

We can meet once again
on a singing rock beach
strewn with shells, seaweed, and debris
a plethora of redolent possibilities
unconventional and spicy presence
like rare frankincense
from the Sahara
or fragrant like erotic orchids
found in a fern forest near Volcanoes National Park.

I You
stuck in a web of gender
move with tentative emotions
you come again
I wait to see your smile
radiant with mine
simultaneous.

Once again touching
evocative traces of Grace shining
soul-dust luminous imbuing our conversations
we will dance
with our tongues and fingers
feet and hands
entranced in a full moon ritual
enhanced by a magic breeze
finally freed at shining season.
Hmmmm. I You. Spicy!

MY SONG

You are hidden
like a star behind the mountain.
You come and go away
but why have you chosen my door?
Your presence runs like music
from sky to sky of my being.

But you are hidden
like the moon behind the cloud
my eyes were caught by your light.
My days are restless
with the south wind blowing.
Storms then stillness pass like a pendulum
reminding me of change in presence.

I know not whether to sing
or remain silent.
With your unknown island of a heart
came the touch of spring
a feeling light and sweet
a fluttering kiss of the breeze
which fell on my being
like a starry veil.

I feel endless
in my joyful knowing.
Your melodies are fresh like the brook
flowing high in the mountain
rushing down past the great banyans
over the weathered stones.

But you stay hidden
so I imagine the touch of your hands
for my pleasure.
Your memory fills my lute
and still there is room to fill.

My song rises to greet you
like the glad bird whose far-spread wings
will touch those whom I meet
who will know you, the stars, and the moon through my song.

RAINBOW VISION

Persimmon passion of bright
Full moon rises   orange
2 hours after gossamer   shower
Vision high   in *Halawa Valley*
Iridescent ribbons of color   kissing the cliffs

Memory of   sitting close to you
Mixing breaths   rubbing noses

Midnight rainbow reveals   shy beauty
across the valley of tears   shimmering

Harmony hides   her modesty
lets fall the secret   of night emotions

Paradox   of shivering showers
and bright beams   of *Hina's* splendor

Magic floats   along the purple *Pali* cliffs
on the high road   past the Stairway to Heaven.

RIDING HIGH

Perched on the high shoulders of your love
I grasp the liana vines of history
and weave garlands of words.

I imagine myself
a night-blooming jasmine
you, the bee, who seizes me with your caress
invading my intimate love treasure
with sweet tender tastings.

You gently pluck me of my senses
the rhapsodies of my flooded heart
correspond to the music of the spheres
my shooting star rides the saddle of your galaxy
announces the fireworks of our celestial dance.

Riding high on the shoulder of your love
I collect fire flowers from the heaven-stretched trees
I hum melodies of pleasure in your ears
spy the secret phoenix
at home high on the torso of mango tree
its mate close by in the purple haze of evening.

After-light fades
faint dewdrops settle on flowers
fireflies begin their trapezoidal dances
and the moon lanterns on the *puakenikeni* blossoms
reveal the tall threshold of our humming love.

You strum sensual rhythms
my undulating waves of passion rise
you magically transform my honey love
to a spiraling dance, red as a *Pinatubo* sunset
and the coming brush of many colors.

I soar then slowly fade
a transformative star of sensations
into the indigo bed of evening's peace
high on the shoulder of your love
dreaming of moonbeams.

ORANGE TOUCH

He came with a golden touch
in the season of orange butterflies

A juggler
with his magic mix
tossing earth and sun rhythms
inserting music
connecting unimaginable possibilities.

In the time of orange butterflies
he put stars in her eyes
movement in her body
fire in her heart and hands
which felt unfamiliar
as a phoenix.

He juggled with notes
connecting rhythms and seeing
new songs responding
balancing breathless harmonies
and days of bright hope.

VALENTINE POEM

Clouds gather in the roseate valley
My world of yours along the singing brook.

We light the patchouli, smudge the sage
Honor the passion under the ancient monkey pod tree
Our lips fold into each other
Perfectly, incomprehensibly beautiful.

I smell the incense of your essence
Love you in bare infinity
We connect by some invisible force
Even as the mists manifest unexpectedly and threaten our clarity.

I follow you
Across the high narrow footbridge
A wire cage wide enough for but one body to pass
Suspended over giant boulders
Tossed like pebbles by the last flooding rains.

We go
Up the path of becoming
Into the unfamiliar evening of passing stars
A barely new moon portends possibilities of another storm.

I hold your hand
On the slippery walk
Up the hidden valley of past lives
Into the hovering clouds.

I sense a sacred force
In the silence of the mountain
Barely detectable as we near
An ancient Hawaiian village
Hidden high behind grandfather trees.

The sky is indigo down by the shore
I love you near the sacred stones
Want to show you what I've got
Dare to give, to share eternity, to amaze.

BRIGHTER THAN VENUS IN HONOLŪLŪ

I saw a meteor
        higher than the apartment complexes
            that scratched the sky
      brighter than Venus in *Honolūlū*
           in the Cancer moon
fall into a great dark thundercloud.

I felt a light
      brighter than love
            that seared my heart
     vaster than the ocean
            that glowed in the night
illuminate my melancholy longing
golden as the autumn sun.

I remembered your sweet presence
      a persistent higher love
transcending the passions of material
        clear as mountain water
insistent as the pounding tides
tender as pure pools.

I breathed blue breaths of gratitude
received the humbling gifts of sparking *akua lele*
          alchemy for the soul.

BEFORE THE RAINS

I visualize your eyes
peering through amorphous feelings
in the fading light of sunset
bright and hopeful like the night ones
who begin their watch as the stars tune in
owls, cats, lovers
companions of the moon who hide
under a coverlet of clouds.
Even in your absence
I feel bathed in a divine light
cool at dusk
just on the other side
of this exquisite moment.
You come to me in this remote spot
smiling at me with your familiar knowing
a myth of romance hidden in the dreamland.

THE QUILT OF OUR LOVE

Quiet is the quilt of our love
like silk splashes of pink clouds
               early at day's first yawn

Quick is the quilt of our love
velvet swatches like soft rabbits
               eager to frolic and fun

Bits of batik, exotic-electric
magic as magnetic taffeta
               everywhere energy

The quilt of our love
quickens the patterns
               stitched fabric dancing to bursting

Reflection on improvisational pieces
of yesterdays, sewn for tomorrow
               patches of red/blue/purple

Clips, cuts, snips, and fragments
from garments worn in the garden
               a pulsing, drumming of colors

The patterns exploding, imploding
expanding, enlivened circles of yellow
               punctuated by white sequin stars

Deep inside the quilt of our love
parameters boundless, cosmogonies infinite
               we are warmed

by the paragon of love's care.

ALL NIGHT LONG

Sunrise and still awake
after all night riding the horse
revved up the universal conch of love
lifted by the fresh song of morning birds
and memory of last night's roaring ocean.

The tender wind passes pauses
caresses the lovers still tangled in semen sheets
The air gentle as a whispered summer breeze
barely noticed
disappears silently reappears
suddenly strong as trade winds before a tropical storm.

Exhaustion humbles
ecstasy spent slumbers quietly
each self dissolved in the heartbeat and pulse of the other
after a rigorous ride.

Sleep comes slowly following all-night passions
the ruby rays of the morning sun
warm the skin and hearts of the lovers
spread the peace of contentment
into the ethers of the coming day.

WAITING FOR DAYBREAK

I am pinks/oranges/reds/persimmons
amid the blue black of night's eye.
I am inspired, restless, sleepless
after Sweet Honey in the Rock, community friends
and a treasured inspiration of fragrant *lehua* blossoms in a *cloisonné* vase.

I listen to Debussy's *Clair de Lune*, Chopin's *Nocturnes*
charming sleep's domain
melodies sweet and gentle float on night-blooming jasmine
freshly fragrant in the *Ka`a`awa* night breeze.

But I elude sleep's magic.
On my flying carpet of memory
I ride out to meet the moon
hastening to your arms and lingering kisses.

This night is quiet as the softest song of crickets
still as a windless abandoned road
mysterious as a star-flung night.

I am all aglow in the wake of our knowing
a fire for the late night's kingdom of silence.
My body tingles and aches for your touch
my solitary hand cannot douse the embers of my desire
and reading cannot distract me from my soulful longing.

Until I see you again, only the great ocean can cool me
comfort me in your absence.
Yet, for her embrace, I must wait for dawn's orchid light.
You are my Harmattan wind, and far away.
I am your star, enflamed by your breath
burning in an endless night.

MYSTIC CHARM

The sea was platinum
the tide was extra low
in the depths of vulnerable emotions
panties pulled down
beneath the moon's impassioned force.

Later, lying in the silver night
I patiently watched the dance
of the charm of clouds
revealing then hiding
the bright face of *Hina*, moon goddess.

The wind laughed raucously
frolicked in the trees
and the tall coconut fronds swayed
in a furious flirt.

The moon's mysterious rainbow
bathed and caressed my naked skin.
The heightened sound of the tide
enchanted my ears
bared by the sound of your absence.

I slept well knowing
the moon is the mystic's charm
a crystal ball substitute
holding secrets of enlightenment
for the observer who is star-kissed
I surrendered
in the arms of the wind
to the embrace of the moon and darkness
surrounded by racing currents and unpredictable tides of light.

FAMILIAR TONGUES

I dreamed you made love to me
under a veil of starlight
spanked me into rhythms
lifted me into the heart
of the golden melody
the essence of the fiery fragrant lotus.

I dreamed we traveled
flying over the sands
to the north of the big waves
contemplating as we passed
the shore break of our lives.

I dreamed
we shared love
on the breeze of forever
riding currents of awesome
talking in tongues familiar
only to us.

ALTERED STATE – LAST NIGHT

Last night
You
Surprised me
As if in my dream.

I heard moon laughter
Happy as clouds
Recurring.
The frolicking air stirred big leaves and Spring branches
Sounds of bamboo and banana trees.

Last night
Dreams enchanted me
On a *bani* ride.
I saw my arm
Recognized your fingers
Savored your touch
Now gentle as a breeze
Next unpredictable and fierce
A piercing desert Mistral.
My breath caught
In my dark breast.
Fullness surprised me.

Last night
I wanted your touch.
You
Spoke in the voice of coconut fronds
Played a subtly bold rhythm
On my hot/cool skin.

I sat close, imagining strong arms
You
Holding me protectively
Unexpected kisses and licks arousing me
Predictable as a sweet melody.

Last night I was happy.

ALTERED STATE – TODAY

Today
In the bold sunlight
You surprised me at the door
An apologetic smile
A flower
A reluctant hug.

I love you
Even when we stumble
Remembering
Today and always
Dreams, dragons
Timeless touching.

ROOM FOR YOU

There is room for you
under the moon
your name known here
in the garden of night-blooming jasmine.

The water in the bay
even the wet sands under my feet
a flutter of touch
your gaze direct as the moon on a clear night
have kept your memory alive.

Many a sailboat passes by this place
of banyan trees growing on the mountainside
but do people notice this spot
on the side of the road
where we lived and touched?

If you must give me your heart
then I will sing—
with me your days will be full of cares
from the high mountains to the deep valleys.

I shall not be made to answer for it
this precious heart of yours
but I will write poems
for how can I remain silent?

Do not ask to understand
when I sing
to your eyes/hands/lips.

Come and walk with me
in the forest of poetry
where the message of moonlight
is written on the leaves.

There is room for you
under the moon
I am dizzy from the trembling memory touching the deep crevices of my heart.

RENEWING OUR VOWS

Pinot Grigio
A vanilla full moon
A taste of fragile emotion
A splash of flirt
A slice of touch
A wedge of deep hugging
I shiver/swoon/falter
Swallow my fear
Enjoy a dash of your romance.

DARKENED ROOMS

Spicy Rides

SASSY ASS

She had a sassy ass
an ass with character
people waited and predicted
men watched her grow
impatient to feel her sassiness
wanting to slide their fingers up and around
make music of it smooth like a trombone
palm over the curve of it like a human gourd
spank it and make it romp like a filly
take it to bed pantiless
work it up to African rhythms
yes indeed
she had a sassy ass
an ass with special character.

MOMENT'S NIPPLE

Singing silence
I sit spread-legged on strong beach.

The Beloved comes
brings heaven together with earth
invisible wedding.

I jump through desire's horizon
feel passion surge with the surf
observe phallic lava rock
          rubbed by shadow of sea grape tree and swarm of honey bees
see bromeliad hiding red neon stamen and pestle.

Ecstasy on nipple
of this moment.

PATCHOULI

I heard a fisherman walk by
the periphery of my morning.
lit my favorite patchouli fragrance
and lay nearly naked
on the faded pink-flowered quilt
watching a translucent gecko
crawl across a termite-damaged wall.

I lay smelling incense
after 2 walks, *taiji*
a splash in the ocean
my body still strong
but winding down.

I lay quietly
sipping mint tea
eating papaya
after bacon and eggs
salsa and chips.

I lay satiated and alone
on the double bed
a coverlet of Indian *madras*
spread like a sun at the foot
my torso draped
in a yellow silk scarf
painted with a stunning fuchsia flower
brought from the art college
in *Xian*, China, where we passed a few sultry days.

I lay star thirsty in patchouli presence
moon crazed
with strong thoughts
and fiery fears
of fragile hearts
and lurking dragons.

LOVE'S SEASONS

Young desire
Hot
Touch
Furnace
Fire
Sweltering forest
Pussy
Undulating
Pulsing
Throbbing
Adult vibrations:
      daily
      weekly
      annual
Perennial hot fertile.

LAUGHTER IN LIGHT

You made my rivers sing
my soul take flight
I followed where you led.

I flew with your fingers
traveling in the mysterious song
of your God-filled caresses.

My goblets I held up for you;
You drank deeply to satisfy your drought.

In the *bani*
I witnessed the waving of wheat fields
the simmering brooks
dancing over the light-filled stones.

Ah, the language of lovers.

CANTOS

I.

My love grows strong
like an ancestral tree in a hidden forest.
My love embraces me like branches
and his limbs become my wedding gown.
He squeezes my nectar
delights in my juices like sweet berries
sucks from my honeycomb until he is satiated.
He ravishes me, leaving me quivering with delight.

The river of my desire
makes the pitchers of my breasts hard
my valleys inviting full of tall waterfalls
that flow to a mighty current.
The moonlight of his caress
awakens me and I rise like a night lily
his touches causing the stars to burst

and sparkle all through and around me.

II.

My love spreads and soars like the joy bird
in tall flight across tropical seas.
I feel endless, breathless
full of fresh life when he is near
my heart losing its limits.

I am like a fragrant *puakenikeni*
my love the warm sun of life
the spice of orange passion.
My flowers fall with the weight of my love.

Enraptured, my love is my light.
His music illumines the far corners of my being
resounds from sky to sky.
In each breath of my sphere
I hear endless melodies, eternally new.

III.

My lover is like the bee
hovering, darting.
I offer him my joys.
My flower flutters at his flirting.
My modesty drops with my clothes.
He takes his fill of sweetness
like a bee on a jasmine blossom at first dawn.

IV.

When he is away, the sun and moon pale.
My love is drained, and there is no music.
The colors fade
my well runs dry
the bird of happiness hides
the blossoms no longer burst open
my heart has neither windows nor doors.

V.

Pleasure is as frail and fleet
as a dewdrop.
Angels of rainbows evaporate
in the harsh light of day.

I mingle my body
with the caress of the night
in a forest of love.
Of all of the flowers
my love has chosen me.

BLUE NOTES

Fly into my indigo cave
up the perfumed mystery of now.

Relax between the pale satin sheets of communion
witness kisses between lovers
nibbles and small bites between breasts thighs lips.

Memory creates erotic blue notes
a rapturous dance in the glass balls of aqua reflection
a captivating melody on mysterious moods
mirrors of sapphire love.

FREAKY

You came to me
cradled me from behind
as I lay sleeping
I felt your hardness
awoke
but you were gone
I smiled the memory of your touch
I breathed the incense of your visit
tasted the lingering
like exquisite Armagnac
or a cup of strong green tea.

GUEST

You let me in
To the door of your heart
I waited patiently
You read *Rumi* to me
I basked in the sun of your love
You massaged my feet
I observed the changing light
You played rhythms in your touch
I read *Rumi* to you
I squeezed my breasts
You remembered an ancient love song
Reading *Rumi* together
We experienced tantric joy
In celebration of the harmony of *Sugmad*.

TOUCHES

Under the shade of a towering tree
your touch sizzles
strong and steady as sunlight.

Your breath and hands
charge like a galloping horse.

Your caress
rides the wind shadows
foreshadowing heavy rains.

SIGHS AND MOANS

Quiet soft
heart kisses resonate
deep to the floor of surrender
moon dances
wind caresses the night
my body rises
even as
the willow tree
outside the window
moans
even as
an orgasm of moonlight
sighs.

CAPE EROTICA

The rocket revs and time accelerates
as heat rises like *Kīlauea* volcano
becoming a rhythmic eruption
into the atmosphere.

Rising like echoes of sea myths
or legends of *Pele*
falling into the embrace of *Kamapua`a*
I fly, lift-off successful.

Momentous energy
rises, falls, sucks, pulls
an ocean break on *Ka`a`awa* thighs of seashore
legs spewed to a sensuous ebb and flow.

Soaring over fiery sands,
I coast high above like an `*iwa* bird
as steel fins send tumultuous heat
propelling past my half-closed eyelids
into my nostrils.

Through the porthole of my fantasy
I hear the songs of the ocean
stroking the guitar of my being
evoking familiar melodies and ancient rhythms.

I shift to an out-of-pattern orbit of imagination
streaking past enormous phallic statues
that pull magnetically
as powerful as the moon on tides.

With love smelling strong like sulfured patchouli
I arc like a meteor
and glide over a steaming valley
where neon rainbows and celestial waterfalls
give brilliant reception
to a successful launch.

INTERNATIONAL INTIMACIES

Here pussy
smell, taste, eat
at the hearth of erotica
slurp it up
my black velvet oyster, my flesh orchid.
Come, come here
time to eat
puss, puss, *poponunu*
cunt yummie milk
piss private.
Come kitty
tush dancer
sit here and rock with me
smell scent
yoni sweet sweet
sacred box secret
genitals natural fragrance *tres* rare.
Improper mutilations incomprehensible
religion, control, dominance
brutal bullying, rough.
We must reach out to help.
Stop! Remember
soft sweet intimacy
marshmallow cream
behind the black veil.
Come back
snatch me
your pussy cat
meow, meow
purr, purr
poochie a moi.
Taste the *toit*
peach wine *tat*
my *punani*, soft pillow
mimi, choochi
chosu, ching ching
fijoka.
Romp in my *kohe*
lepelepe like magic
flying vagina

inspiring *lina*
my wild bush.
Rest, relax
in "that thang"
the nappy dugout
ha, ha, ha.
Seek once more
the exotic cave
my bean
my coffee *vidachi*
my early morning sweetie
my mango juice.
Here kitty kitty
the day has flown
come once more
take my late-night guava cocktail
sweet and sour
my *bilat*, my pussy
purr purr
drift with me to dreamtime
on the pillow of my delight.

HAPPY YOU AND I

Dancing
Bumping
Spooning
Thumping
Waltzing
You and I.

Laughing
Pouting
Smiling
Shouting
Swaying
Paying
You and I.

Tripping
Skipping
Tipping
Lipping
Flipping
You and I.

Hoping
Coping
Waiting
Praying
Loving
Affirming
You and I.

SLOW DOWN THE TEMPO

Slow down the tempo
my love warrior
your passion stronger than the midday sun
intenser than Sahara heat
caress me
once again
my Sweet
soft and slow
to the ocean of bliss
rock me
to surrender
so tender
soft waves of touch on my golden shore
your rhythms of love captivate
ohhh, ooooh, wheeee
go deeper with me
touch me
there.

QUIET SOFT DEEP

Quiet heart remembers soft
deep kisses on bed of emotions
resonates rhythms regular, familiar.

Nostalgia evokes sensory moon dance
on deep piles of silver shimmer leaves.

Subtle wind arises
caresses limbs and branches.

A soul sighs on the carpet of grass
beneath the willow tree
outside my open window.

Pines moan on the hillside nearby
I feel you enter my being
and poems drop with my love.

YELLOW JOY

We woke up
drenched in passion
place and time irrelevant
gilded flowers burst open
in mind and body.
Moisture dried out
in the slow lemon sun of the morning.

The golden ginger was not in bloom
still our yellow joy filled the day.

PAYMENT

I hang on the ragged edge of fatigue
Somehow savoring it as payment
After sensitive caresses and sweet kisses
Resting in your arms, under the half-moon glow.

Engulfed in your warmth, in your tenderness
I feel like a fresh-blooming *puakenikeni*
Waiting to be plucked again by your loving
Oblivious to the cooling fragrant breeze.

VOLCANO

I.

On a crater's edge
We meet once more
Kiss taste touch
Explore nibble
Suck the nectars of knowing
Hot rivers slowly bubble
flow, torch the tall trees.

Passing through this national park
Pause and follow intuition
Sit still on rough rock of cooled glass lava
Hardened in air and time
Observe the remnants of black flows
Trail over the cliffs to ecstatic surrender
Fall down toward anchorage and the embracing sea.

No riddle
Wetness calls to the heat
Release at last
Flows beyond blockage into brightness
We create a lighted path
Beyond blockage
Toward greater understanding
Nature's grandeur, organic laws.

II.

Wake up to rain shower
The fertile truth of welcoming water
That cools the lover's soul
On the rim of *Halema`uma`u* crater
Summer hoodoo breeze sings of early morning joy
Refreshes romance
Lovers flirt and play
Still untouched by day's requirements.

Witness powerful energies
That float up and around the feeding family
Of rare *nēnē* birds meandering near the unpredictable volcano.

QUELL THE PASSIONS

Touch me
quell the passions
      which storm my being
subdue the epochal flames
      which blaze like suns, meteors
      moons, and stars.

HALLOWEEN AND HARVEST MOON

"One does not discover new lands without consenting
to lose sight of the shore for a very long time." André Gide

More terrifying
than the strange creature
of imagination
from which we get
all our shadows and doubts
I stood
witch-rooted
in my private suite of memories
images pressed on images
elusive cottage of many seasons.

Whatever I did
wherever I went
you were always with me
fluttering at the edges of my dreams
and desires
like I had met you
in another world
you made such a strong song
pulse in my blood.

Will you be
my boo
this Halloween
under the Harvest moon?

SHORE BREAK

There is a canoe of many sails
on the horizon of the blue-hued ocean.
I think of you and wonder
where and how
your sweet essence is floating.

Oceans of separation
time like dreams
beyond the wall of paradigms
and orderly boundaries.

With you
harmony flows like persuasive water
and melody waltzes with the shore break
cymbals then sea spray
as you come and go.

A soft presence
beckons in aquamarine whispers.
Generations gather invisibly
like souls over a clear surface.

Baptism in love
and many I's follow
the fading sails
beyond the protection of the reef.

ABSENCE OF FORM

The Mystery of Longing

LEDGE

I missed you this morning
I came after the roosters finished crowing
but you were already in another place
galloping on a steed of cosmos
visiting the galaxies beyond time.

So I went walking
on the hillside
and you came on the wind
under partly cloudy star-breath
invisible in the bright sun.

I contemplated faces
while sitting on the stone ledge
high behind the house
and for a minute
I was intoxicated.

I heard and saw harmonies
subliminal as a sweet fragrance
in the perfumed garden.

I let go and floated
beyond gravity
we touched
connected out of time
beyond reason
and when I came back to the wall
I was glowing golden-red
like a lotus
in a sparkling pond of clear water.

Still I missed seeing your smile
in person
but felt
the wind blow light
across the hillside
I remembered the dark of the new moon
when we walked out together
and you kissed me goodnight
under the towering pines and the luminescent stars.

YOUR FACE

I saw
your face
anxious
as if
in
a bad dream
I had been
away
far
so had you
the dragon moon
harvest orange
clouded
by many
doubts

I saw
your eyes
passing squalls
gone
the playful
spirit
dancing faith
of former days
no longer
welcome

I reached out
and found
an empty
ghost
then woke up
you
no longer
near
only
bones of a nightmare.

WILLOW TREES AND BULLWHIP SNAKES

Hauntingly dark
by the sleepy river
thoughts perched in the crotch of a willow tree
fighting fears of bullwhip snakes

Rainbow tears
shattered hopes and slithering pain
fall through deep cold holes of emotions

Romance
passes like seasons
a waltz of ago
at the end of the darkening sky on the banks of no return
I note the absence of your surprises.
Communication becomes unpredictable
as stormy waters hide camouflaged serpents of doubt.

TORCHES

Torches and ghosts
fly inside
her mind
like bats.

Hungry sufferings
A heart swallowed
            by emptiness.

Absence parades
even as trees perform
sky songs
high in the mountains.

She can hardly remember
the color
            of his touch
the fire
            of his voice
the smell
            of his hair.

Ghosts of memories
hold her
hungering.
He is irrevocably absent
an unlit torch
in a prison of absence.

SOLITUDE'S LAMENT

Birds greet the day
like my bracelets' tingling song
and from dawn's first breath
I wait expectantly.

The wind brushes and caresses
the blossom-burdened trees
ruffles the waves which kiss and part
from the shore.

The clouds have come,
the majestic rain of age advances.
Gleefully the trees dance
in the rain's reviving breaths.

A fruit is not so sweet when green;
a love is not so shallow when mature.
I see clear moonbeams beyond my cloudy emotions
revealing the paradox of my presence.

Clusters of stars adorn the night
a diadem complimenting
the satin gown of moonlight
I stay alone, hoping for love.

My lips remain un-kissed, my bosom
untouched, my arms and bed empty.
I sit in fragrance as the moon moves
unfulfilled and deserted by the fates.

I contemplate separation and solitude
beneath the sheltering parasol of clouds
trying to remember the rainbow's arch
beyond the illusion of happiness.

NETS NOT YET SWALLOWED

Global gray lingers
while I am missing you on the shore
in the sky corners of my sea-space.

Stormy winter tides
deposit nets
not yet swallowed
by porpoises/dolphins/whales.

The large golden beach
becomes debris-strewn and deserted
like my heart.

TELEPHONE NOTES

Holding a long memory
and awakened to a new daring,
I called you on the telephone
and no one was at home.

I imagined a conversation
of rising cycles
dancing moon shadows
on a cold evening's passing.

But when I called to you,
there was no answer.
Or was it that I heard differently
on the other side of the mountain?

I had seen a vision:
A pageant of stars
symbols in a celestial field
offering a shimmering hope of full expectation.

I felt good, so I called you on the telephone,
remembering our nuptial vows,
surrounding the waltz-of-we at dawn's melody,
but no one was at home.

I wondered who was watching the dance with whom,
and from what realm trilled the notes.
Who were the choreographers?
Still there was no answer beyond my inner balcony.

Now I call again on the swaying wire,
sending a message of reminiscence,
braving the cold currents,
And hoping that you will hear.

THAT YOU WERE HERE

Alone in a circle of self's creation
Clear space with crystals, herbs, roots
Incense, books, tarot cards
Mists dance in sacred silence
Along the peaks nearby
Wind symphony evokes romantic excursions
Cliff visions accompany high notes
Melody of Chopin
Trills wistful.
We together cuddled
In the darkening chill.

A surprise shower passes
Cools the lavender evening.

I hear an insistent pounding
Beyond my door
Dance of surf on coral reefs
Sharp and hard edges
Reverberate remembrance.

Beyond the rugged emptiness
Purple ridges rise
The omnipresent *Ko`olau* mountain range looms
Your memory rides a tall phallic cliff.

Will you come to me now
In my crystals
On an aura of rebirth
Walk up the familiar trail where I wait
Behind the singing rock beach
Can you appease my fears
Satiate my longing?

BIRD'S VIEW

High up on Mt. Tantalus
With you so far away
I trust and see in trees.

Gliding on a bird's view
Eucalyptus and tall shadows
      stretch your absence
As the sun lounges on mirrored water
      off *Honolūlū* Harbor.

Within a platinum sea of emotions
You seem so far away
      in the talons of another's presence.

Impoverished
Seeking solace in the regions of my love
I flee to the hills
      hating my rival.

Cars and trucks
Occasionally pass by and stop
      like mosquitoes
Violating my stillness
      fragmenting the colorful prism of sensitivity.
The men in them seem to be intruding
      upon my solitary flight.

I depart their subtle advances
As down on the horizon ships move across
      a slice of my vision
Sailing to unknown destinations.

Flying high again
I find solace in the fragrances
      of lofty heights
Soaring on the currents of wind
      and birdsong
Seeking the regions of my love.

RISKY BUSINESS

Here I am again
Moonstruck
Riding my broom of intuition
Hanging out in dreams
Mine and yours.

Alone, here I am
Night twinkles
Star dust on tall banana leaves
Magic hums all around the church of love.

I follow dirt roads
Like forgotten paths
Avoiding monsters
Helped by elves
Moon dances on dark skin
And white stones
Music leads incrementally.

Solitary life soars on a wing of presence
Life dives on the scorching breath
Of hidden sleeping dragons
Lurking off familiar.

BEING ALONE

Venus appeared early and alone
persistent between the clouds
before I walked through the green glen
of the dirt road
beyond the ironwoods
and spirit of the elder trees
the wind sang me
a love song
reminding of past joys
and star-flung dreams.

LAST NIGHT I DREAMED

Last night I dreamed
I saw you standing there
with moonlight in your hair
like before, evermore.

In the evening wind
I heard you call my name
Your voice sounded the same
like before, evermore.

While the moon was there
I felt you touch my face
in our special place
like before, evermore.

Late last night, near dawn
at a magic hour
I smelled the flowers
all alone, all alone.

Last night I dreamed
I danced to "Pua Hone"
aloha to my one and only
cried a tear, you were not here
nevermore, nevermore.

SITTING AND WAITING

Sitting and waiting
Waiting and sitting
Wondering when
We'll be together again.

Yearning and waiting
Waiting and yearning
Inside a burning
How has it changed?

Distance and silence
Silence and distance
Not like arranged
The ideal love play.

Closeness a habit
Habit in closeness
How long can it be
This separate necessity?

I miss your twinkle
Long for your touch
Where do I turn
When I miss you so much?

The love I share
Will always be there
My heart is open
Though I be long gone.

My song I give to you
To you I sing
From the best of my glass house
My heart I bring.

TINY SHELL

I returned again
across the earth-tones lava rock
to our favorite cove
where the river meets the sea
and the waves are hurled off the jagged reef.

Thinking of you,
I picked up sea shells
black ones with blue pearl iridescence
shattered cowries
thrown upon a barren coast.

I found the tiniest of shells
hardly noticeable
and identified with my insignificance
in your space.

NEW YEAR

Purples and eventide
I am alone with the cobalt shore
The ocean speaks in whispers
Listen.

Where are you, my friend?
During this time of war, earthquakes, and suffering
Rescues and successes
Huge scale of mighty mysteries
Failures and movements
Changes in seasons
New riddles of environmental balance shifts.

We rarely communicate
Materialism before sincerity
You no longer in the bed of my heart.

Perennial questions. Who am I? What to do?
How to heal my indigo soul?

I listen to celestial correspondences
Watch the years and hear the waves
Answers always invisible side by side.

YOUR SAX

Rhapsody on a saxophone
memories of you
split lip and worrying
waiting to get back
to your old lady
your real love
your horn.

Jazz skipped
from your fingers of soul
through your lips
alive, and variable
like winds in January
insistent as Coltrane
strident as *bebop*.

Your energy rushed by
like the crazed wind
a whirling riff
high to low
plunging, piercing, penetrating
creating ecstasy
not to be repeated
ever again in the same way.

Was it a dream?
Am I still seeking you?
Sometimes,
your riffs and magic tunes
seemed sweet unto tears
like starlight to my ears.

I have never forgotten
your kiss of music
you and me
together creating
under the jazz of starlight
and melody of a passing moon.

Echoes of your sax
imprint my being.

WAITING AGAIN

I keep waiting
for your return
the silver moon waxes and wanes
the tides ebb and flow
the `iwa birds come and go
with each passing storm.

And I
a flower waiting for the seed
keep patiently waiting
for your return.

I listen for the sound
of your return
your voice
your laughter
in the rising surf
in the winter winds.

I dreamed that you were here
again I felt your touch
as surely as the wind
smelled your body
as surely as the ginger blossoms
which bloomed this morning
outside my window.

I keep waiting
and smiling
knowing we will meet again soon.

YOUR SMILE

I rode the *bani* of shimmering light
        big blue waves of presence
        spontaneity surging on towering crests
        splashes moving in and out.

I recognized your smile
        familiar near the shore of surprise
        a teasing hide and seek
        behind the ironwood trees.

I heard turquoise laughter
        imagined your golden touch
        asked how long before
        we surf together again?

THE TANGLE OF OUR PAST

I remember passionately
the dateless tangle of our past
a collage of emotions
colorful as Brazilian parrots
fragrant as Hawaiian flowers
turbulent as a tussled bed
imbroglio of our love.

This evening
your absence throbs like an amputation.
I am full of a colorless malaise
a longing for our exotic treasure
of togetherness.

Instead
I feel the empty expanse of a deserted landscape
a fading sunset and an unfamiliar north wind.

EARLY MORNING

Once again
You have come and gone.
The sun of your being
lit the sphere of my melody.

My emotions tinkle
a thousand tiny bells
remembering your touch.

I greet the early morning dazzle
pick fresh figs and gather *puakenikeni*
for my untamed hair.

But their taste and smell
seem wan and subdued
in your cloudy absence.

SPIRALING INCENSE

I mourned your passing from the bed of my heart
as I lay between indigo sheets in dark puddles of tears,
mourned the letting go, my naked body aching
for your familiar touch, your words dripping honey.

I lamented the void left by your voice
each time you called my name.
But was it only when you needed me
and not when I needed you too?

I mourned your passing from the bed of my heart
as I sat by the window watching white hibiscus
bloom and die three times, since last I heard
your footsteps on the path.

I languished near the phone, expectantly
like a child, for days, weeks, seasons
believing your ardor sprouted from the illusive garden of love.
I grieved that you knew me so little.

I mourned your passing from the bed of my heart
that rainy October evening of frankincense and cloud-gathering,
and I prepared to face the spiraling years
alone with the beasts of aborted dreams.

I mourned as I prepared for an empty caravan
crossing the Sahara of my being.

GOOD FORTUNE

Separation and Liberation

BEYOND THE MATERIAL WORLD

Beyond the material world
I live uncensored
in the golden currents of life.
I swim freely
in intimate flutes and tinkling bells
above the blare of the cement city.

Moments empty
of inner abundance and green joy
the peace of this place dwells
beyond the material world
transcends differences and cultures
lingers not with doubt and mistrust
clings not to tomorrow's hope.
Yet in the emptiness of now
I rest content.

Beyond the material world
I ride a carpet of inspiration
on a wind of forever
to a place almost forgotten
deep within my flowing soul.
Here I can rest and dwell for a while
beyond expectations and inspection
requirements, regulations, obligations.
I can dwell for a while
in my inner room
lit by love bright as the sun
beautiful as the lotus flower
soothing as the summer moon.

Beyond the material world
I transcend time and space
uncensored and free.
Eternity is now.
God is now.
Beyond the material world
the past and the future do not exist
except in illusive memories and dreams.

CONTEMPLATION

As the advancing day reveals
a rapidly expanding skyline
bamboo scaffolding
horizontal slats across ladder poles
10 stories tall
thick like forest farms
endless blocs
of ordered cement housing
framed by the sky over *Beijing*
I sit and remember
when you made love to me
or did I only imagine
such tenderness
bewitched by the China sky.

CROSSING

It was a time
beyond boundaries
my being flooded with joy
awe at ancient origins
carrying the days in my hands
like precious jewels
I explored temples
perched high on mountain ridges
above the China sea.

6,000 CRANES

Except for the gray gritty air
Beijing could be New York
Except for the 6,000 cranes
Beijing could be Paris
Except for the million dancing night lights
Everywhere a glitter, every color, design, and art
Beijing could be Moscow
Except for the flowers and tree-lined freeways
Beijing could be Los Angeles
Except for the music and walled *hutong* communities
Beijing could be Athens
Except for the fabulous *Sichuan* chicken
Beijing could be Dallas
Except for the 6 story walk-ups
Beijing could be *Honolūlū*
Except for the city of 17 million people
Beijing could be home.

MT. LAOSHAN AFTER THE SNOWS

The triumphant profusion of plum blossoms
Reminds her of you
With beauty and power.

Summer in *Qingdao*
Peaches and plums in abundance
A mysterious veil of mist
Plays between the jade mountain
And the dancing sea.

Small gatherings of learned people
Ponder and create in a glen of pines
Beside a long river
Flowing out of time
From a remote source.

The woman takes a seldom-used path
To a tall waterfall
Chants a poem for you
Accompanied by the music of water flowing
At Mt. *Laoshan* after the snows.

Lotus blossoms paint the pool below
Red dragonflies tease with shimmering wings
Graceful in the face of a strong wind
And green cypress trees bear witness
To generations of a changing China.

Later at *Fa Da* Mansion
She passes the evening with generous friends
Eating mussels, drinking plum tea, and wishing you were here.

COUNTRYSIDE

Take a look.

From the shoreline
Laoshan's mist
Hides the stunning beauty of the mountains
The rugged terrain
Giant stone formations
Tattooed with red calligraphy and poems
Small waterfalls and rocky riverbeds.

Go closer.

The clear smiles of the farmers
The music of their voices
The myriad tastes of fresh fish
And succulent dishes prepared to perfection
Offerings of beer and wine
Abundant as a spring river
As peaches, apricots, and cherries
Harvested on the hillsides of *Laoshan* in June
Are sold along the country road, near the new freeway.

Admire *Laoshan*.

The generosity of her residents
The love in the families and our hosts
Warm and open like a sunny day
All assure the visitors' speedy return to the countryside.

CURRENTS OF IMAGINATION

The sun of my imagination
creates sharp lines and a retreat called umbra
where my moon resides.
Umbra permits periodically the currents of passage
to penetrate my vagina
of survival's necessity.

Inspiration passes through umbra
deep currents of breath and water
necessary for creativity
waiting to be collected.
The golden moments of being.

Currents reveal themselves in the organic weaving of years
adorned with lacy thoughts and tunes
filigreed moments to communicate
intricate meanings in life's seasons.

A covetous river of mechanical thought
unexpectedly meets the deceptive rapids,
turbulent white water swirls out of control.
Inspiration hesitates and tries to turn back
when faced with the possible:
splashes of laughter, whirlpools of tragedy
the coming experience of explosive intensity
ecstasy of the unknown.

The lugubrious muddy river of mechanical mind
learns the lessons of play
and humor through surrender
liberation of flow, upheavals, juxtapositions
contradictions, clarity, miracles
water evaporates up, only to fall down
to an otherwise inaccessible destination.

The currents of a loving universe
mirrored on earth
shimmer on the leaves/trees/oceans
creating music: hums, chants, billions of songs
carried by organic life: whales, *honu*, kelp
in the sea canyons
voices and sounds vibrating celestial harmonies from there to here—
currents of imagination: visible, audible, perceptible

CONJURE

Conjure from nature
Sun saturated
Plump raisins
Altar of intoxication
Offering to the Gods
Evoking dreams
Beseeching answers to perennial questions
Demystifying hoodoo.

WAITING TOGETHER

My grandchild and I while away the afternoon
under the mantle of shade
offered by the tall *Ka`a`awa* ironwood trees.

Watching her go for a swim
I move closer into the sun
and startle a fisherman
dreaming on the rocks
near the false *kamani* tree.

When I return to the shadows
my granddaughter is tired and still
stretched out on her Nautica beach towel
flung across a large hot flat stone.

We sit in silence and rest
no lists
no phones
no web
no work
no plan
just being and waiting together.

ARCHEOLOGICAL DIG

Unearthing fickle memory
patterns of personal
fragments of dirt discarded
forgotten.

Discovering occasional diamonds
rare gems of presence
mines of precious pleasures
forgotten.

Love tablets and happy times
tucked away carefully
in a box hidden underneath the worn mattress of time
forgotten.

Archeological recovery
a beautiful *stela*
of conscious moments
golden calligraphy of essence
revelation no longer forgotten.

GOOD FORTUNE

See the jeweled vision of my heart
The glistening pearls of presence
Selectively strung and knotted with care.

Beloved,   "Be."

Excite the twittering birds of my love with your laughter
Above the bench of my nearness.

Beloved,   "Beware."

Beyond the celebration of my awareness
Hear the deep thunder of uncertainty
Sky's warning laughter against my ear
Twitching wakefulness and conscience.

Beloved,   "Be aware."

You next to me
The curtain of intimacy behind us
Ecstatic, I bow
Before the infinite fields of love
The singing emotions.

Beloved,   "Be still."

The fragrant candles
Inspire a whirling chance of attention
Choice sacred
Holy moments.

Beloved,   "Be the gift."

Hot blaze of sunlight
Shimmers on bright breeze
Burgundy *plumeria* blooms vibrant
On thin branch of instinctive
The lovers slowly yield to the passing
The cooling passions
Surrender to the evening wind's soft music.

Beloved,   "Be grateful."

HAIKU

I.
The singing moon's song
Lights the ears of my love
Hear the happy lute.

II.
Ti leaf touch cools
Rain on tropical leaves
Feeling of healing.

III.
Hopes and fears unmask
Helpless tears masquerade
Minds of many ghosts.

IV.
Erotic melody excites
Behind night screen of moon's Muse
Passion notes exhaust.

V.
A music blessing
Wings its way to my body
You play heaven's song.

THE MYSTERY OF BEES

Bees suck honey from *lehua* blossoms
High splashes of volcanic red delicacies on jade-green leaves.

Bees hum all around `*ōhi*`*a* trees
Rimming the steaming volcano, sprouting from rough lava.

Bees sting the inattentive wanderer
Bringing unnecessary suffering along an unpredictable path.

METAMORPHOSIS

Magic of cocoon process
alchemy of larvae
dark growth, hidden away
then transformation—
emerge the *pulelehua* butterfly
kissing the flowering trees!

Pale colors, intricate designs pop out:
purple, orange, white, yellow
bordered by black.
Grace dances flutters in blue air
springtime metamorphosis
just beyond my fingertips.

FLOWER SEDUCTIONS

The pale green leaves curtain the dawn
The exotic flowers open their white yellow and pink blouses
Their bodies welcome the bees and butterflies.

The bees and butterflies find them
Beautiful
      Fragrant
           Tasty
Iridescent desire flashes
A fiery sun rises catching them
      Drinking deeply
      Sliding deeper into their wells of life
           The sticky soul of the sweet flowers.

Do bees and butterflies know death?
We humans are sometimes too fearful
In everything, even behind the sweetest kisses
Death watches
Waiting for weakness
Anywhere.

Do bees and butterflies know love?
The endless faith of flagrant forever
The heartless gift.

Do the flowers spend their honey
To the sucking butterflies and bees
Who repay with their process of pollination?
Ah, the simplicity.

RITUAL RETURNS

Each morning
Thank the ritual return of each day
Thank the pearly grey doves
Cooing softly
Thank the green parrots
Early morning flight across the *Ko`olau* mountains
Thank the noisy roosters
Alarm for the day.
Thank each evening
Thank the Indonesian thrush's
Song of a nightingale
Fluttering in low branches
Ruffling the lavender air
Thank songs, sputters, warbles, flutters
Varying voices, vigors, colors, sounds, songs
Lounging in the changing light
Floating by the gauzy curtain of sleep and dreams.

GATHERING GLASS

At 5:00 am, the moon rode silver on sea spray
through the window of the beach house.
I awoke with a BURP, BELCH alarm
energized, ready to go out alone to the sunrise beach
and brave the sea stars and unfamiliar shadows.

Instead, I went into the great living room,
stretched out on the time-forsaken couch,
my head pressed against the window pane like a child's
wondered why the moon was calling me so intensely, insistently.

I read the first lesson in the Book of Miracles.
I gathered my fears and deliberately put them aside,
walked out to the chill away from *Makaloa* Point
to look for glass balls which might have survived the recent storm
and ridden to the shore by *Mokuli`i* island
on the gusty wind and storm-flung waves.

The moon seemed less than half full
as it neared the western horizon of foreboding mountain peaks,
yet due to the earth's shadow
it magically cast a perfect circle
which followed me like a friend
as I walked down the rocky coastline.

Periodically, my flashlight revealed assorted shapes and sizes
of clear, green, and brown glass bottles,
assorted debris, strewn haphazardly on the lonely beach.
I gathered a dozen
into my woven African bag.

Almost a mile down the beach,
I was ready to turn back,
just past the night fishermen,
when my flashlight caught a reflection of moonlight
on a rounded green sphere,
floating at the water's edge.

At first I doubted—
it had been 10 years since I had found the last gift.
I walked closer, braving the surf,
and to my exhilaration
I grabbed a wet, barnacle-covered glass ball
the size of a Japanese pear,
a circle of luck, an oracle of good fortune,
there for me from the Muse of Creativity.

Later, back at the house,
the blown ball,
formerly a float for fishing nets,
seemed perfect for divination
or inspiration.

I placed it by a window facing the sea,
on the *koa* coffee table,
next to my crystal pyramid,
to radiate its mysterious energy
and irregular turquoise beauty.

WIDER VISION

Music in poems
music in stones
music in trees

Dreams and desires
touching, kissing
dreams and desires

Music in dreams
music in kisses
Where does it lead?

Surrender to sky
change of view stretches
let go, let go

Music in laughter
music in tears
salty rainbows

Let go the trivial
unknown notes
swinging on dreams

Attach to no more
no thing, no desire
let music flow fresh

Bird sings morning
hummingbird dances alone
music in trees
music in poems
music in stones
music in tears.

RECIPE FOR TRANSFORMATION

Ingredients
Attention
Observation
Remembering
Transform in a start

Add
Each moment
Your self
Your place
Your life
Present yourself for Baptism of clarity
A wish on a shooting star

Stir gently and thoroughly
Love and attraction
Exploration and discoveries
Sacred beauty of now
Family and friends

Bake
A lifetime
Shower abundance
All around

Serve
Wake up in love's arms
Sunny embrace of today

EACH DAY

awake
feel
give thanks
walk in the garden
look
sit
ponder
see
forgive
decide
commit
move
adjust
continue
complete
rest

        all in silence
grateful
        for life and for love

LADDER

I keep seeking a pure day
affirmative in each stirring of the wind
in the willows
in each sun sparkle on the sea.
But instead I get questioning notes
all around my scale of melodies
down the basement steps of yesterday
up the bell tower of tomorrow.

A pure affirmation perhaps exists
only in the realm of angels
who hold the keys to golden dreams
and answers true.

I follow the path of the flitting white butterfly
circuitous and magical
seeking the pure day
to live freer than the thousands
of delighted students finishing classes
at the end of a semester
freer than the burdened professors
and tired blue-collar workers
freer than the rich businessmen
and their illimitable servants
all purposeful
but no longer spontaneous
nor mindful of joy.

I keep seeking a pure day
a companion to my most daring emotions
in the spring of promises
but instead
I get quizzical stares
stony silence which melts to welcome me
when I remember to smile.

I go up
turn and watch a bird in flight
marvel at his song rising
even in the threatening sky.

What unbridled notes burst forth,
or is it as mechanical
as our melancholy moments
in the trill of summer's season?

Up the ladder of consciousness
I get a sense of being a part
of some larger fleeting process
perennial and international transformation
of life on the planet.

I keep seeking a pure day
again and again I return
to the unfettered flight
of the dark butterfly
the soaring bird
the rising note
in a microcosm of time
affirming life on earth
in the wind, in the breath
that nurtures
in the flower that inspires
in the ocean of light
in the fire of presence.

WALKING SPIRIT

Feet on earth
balanced, walk on

walk into a new soul
a new dream
a new rhythm
walk beyond
buses, trains, cars, trucks
walk the whole body
walk up and down
to the sea, in the woods, off the path
up the mountain, down the hill to the neighbors
in the community, through mazes
through the ancient temples

walk a meditation
feel your feet
connect, channel
walk on

develop a callous or three
walk on

wear out shoes
create your own soles
walk on

walk to see the Beloved
in fields of light
walk with parents, family
friends, or just
with the memory of the ancestors
walk with lovers
walk in the spirit

walk on.

GLOSSARY

Adderly, Julian Edwin

Julian Edwin "Cannonball" Adderly (1928-1975) was an American jazz alto saxophonist popular in the 1950s and 1960s.

akua lele

In Hawaiian mythology, this is a ghost, specter, apparition, or evil spirit.

aloha

A greeting commonly used in the Hawaiian islands. It can also mean affection or sympathy.

Anderson, C. Alfred

C. Alfred "Chief" Anderson (1907-1996) was an American aviator. Training black pilots for the U.S. Army at the Tuskegee Institute in the 1940s, he is known as the Father of Black Aviation.

bani

Used in Eckankar spiritual practice, it means shimmering light to heaven.

banyan

A large East Indian tree found in Hawai`i with branches that send out shoots which grow down to the soil to form secondary trunks.

Beijing

The capital of the People's Republic of China.

belissimo

Beautiful, lovely, gorgeous, in Italian.

Beloved

The endless source from which all energy flows. God, Creator, Sugmad.

Book of Miracles

Psychologist Helen Schucman said that she wrote *A Course in Miracles* under the influence of visions and dreams provided by "an inner voice" she called Jesus. Others helped her revise the book, published in 1976.

Carver, George Washington

George Washington Carver (1864-1943) was an African American botanist, scientist, and educator. A noted inventor, he discovered new uses for peanuts, soybeans, and sweet potatoes. In 1941, Time Magazine named him "the black Leonardo."

Catherine the Great

Also known as Yekaterina II (Catherine II) and Yekaterina Alexeevna. Catherine the Great (1729-1796) was the longest-ruling woman monarch leading Russia. Her name is also Anglicized as Katherine the Great and Kathryn the Great. Born in Prague, she reigned after the assassination of her husband, Peter III. Under her reign, Russia became a great power.

Chopin, Frédéric François

Frédéric François Chopin (1810-1849) was a Polish piano composer who settled in Paris at age 21 and preferred performing in the intimate settings of small artistic salons rather than for large (commercial) public audiences.

"Clair de Lune"

The French term for moonlight, this is the third movement from Claude Debussy's piano composition Suite bergamasque. Debussy's "Clair de Lune" musically depicts Paul Verlaine's poem of the same title.

cloisonné

An ancient technique for decorating metal, more recently with enamel. Especially popular with the Chinese.

"Le Coeur m'en seigne"   A phrase from a French novel, Elle seigne á la lantern, by Paul Sanda. My poem "Moon Rituals" plays with this phase.

Coltrane, John William   John William Coltrane (1926-1967) was an American jazz saxophonist noted for bringing together jazz musicians to perform and record jazz music. He influenced numerous musicians. He turned increasingly towards spirituality in his life and work.

Confucius   Confucius (551-471 BCE) was a Chinese philosopher, educator, and politician credited with writing or editing many of the Chinese classic texts including the Five Classics. Confucian principles included respect for elders and ancestor worship, among others. He recommended the family as a model for government to follow. His students and followers organized his teachings into the Analects, expanding on his ideas in a series of elaborate rules and practices.

cosmogony   Any theory concerning the origin of the cosmos.

Le Côte d'Ivoire   A nation in West Africa also known as the Ivory Coast.

Debussy, Achille-Claude   Achille-Claude Debussy (1862-1918) was a French composer of impressionist music.

Delta Sigma Theta   Founded in 1913, Delta Sigma Theta is a historically black sorority for college women dedicated to programs uplifting African Americans. Before 1965, U.S. segregation laws mandated that minorities and whites could not join the same fraternal organizations, so African Americans established their own groups, such as this one. Today, persons of any race may apply to join any fraternity or sorority.

Fa Da Mansion

A tourist attraction and restaurant in Qingdao, China, located near Laoshi Park.

false kamani tree

There are two types of kamani trees in the Hawaiian islands: true kamani and false kamani. In the Mangosteen family, true kamani was introduced with the early Polynesian settlers and is also known as Alexandrian laurel. A common tropical almond, false kamani became established after the first white settlers arrived.

gecko

A type of lizard found in warm climates throughout the world. The Hawaiian islands have eight gecko species, all of which are non-native.

Gide, André

André Paul Guillaume Gide (1869-1951) was a French author who won the Nobel Prize in 1947. His writing focused on growth of the soul.

ginger

A sweet-smelling flower (called awapu`hi in Hawaiian), yellow or white in color, often used for lei making. Another variety of the ginger root is used for cooking and medicinal purposes.

haiku

A very short Japanese poem following prescribed rules of construction.

Ha`ikū

See Stairway to Heaven.

Hālawa

An area on the island of Moloka`i including a valley and waterfalls.

Halema`uma`u Crater A currently active pit crater of Kīlauea Volcano in Hawai`i Volcanoes National Park, with lava erupting in an open vent. In Hawaiian mythology, this crater is the home of the goddess Pele.

Harmattan A dry, dusty West African trade wind blowing northeasterly from the Sahara Desert into the Gulf of Guinea between November and March.

**Hawai`i, Big Island**  The largest of the eight major islands of Hawai`i. The other islands are Kaho`olawe, Kaua`i, Lana`i, Maui, Moloka`i, Ni`ihau, and O`ahu.

hibiscus A genus of large shrubs and small trees in the Mallow family cultivated to attract butterflies, bees, and humming-birds. The plant exists nearly everywhere in the world, and human beings have developed many uses for it, such as tea, candy, and paper. The flower has no odor but comes in various shapes, sizes, and colors. It is the Hawai`i State flower.

Hina The goddess of the moon in the native Hawaiian religion.

Honolūlū The city of Honolūlū located on the island of O`ahu is the capital of the State of Hawai'i.

honū The Hawaiian word for turtle.

hoodoo African American traditional folk magic.

hutong Narrow streets or alleys in northern Chinese cities, especially Beijing. Also small walled-in housing compound, usually associated with extended family.

Indonesian thrush

In the thrush family, the island thrush is a common forest bird. With nearly 50 subspecies, it is prevalent throughout southeast Asia and the Pacific. A subspecies from Indonesia is undergoing scientific description.

`iwa

This is the Hawaiian name for Great Frigatebird, which is known for its opportunistic feeding behaviors. Feeding mainly by snatching flying fish from the air or smaller fish pushed to the surface by larger fish, like all frigatebirds they never land on the water's surface. The females are known to steal and eat chicks from the nests of other seabirds. These birds also practice kleptoparasitism, chasing other seabirds until they regurgitate their food, and then eating the regurgitated food. In Hawaiian, `iwa means "thief." This bird often appears in Hawaiian mythology.

Japanese pear

A tree species native to East Asia, Pyrus pyrifolia is called Asian pear, Chinese pear, Japanese pear, Korean pear, apple pear, and sand pear. They have a high water content, grainy texture, and sugary taste.

jasmine

A genus of shrubs and vines in the olive family cultivated for their sweet smell.

Jim Crow

Racial segregation laws enacted in the U.S. between 1876 and 1965.

Jubilee songs

During the slavery period, African Americans developed songs of unity and uplift known as spirituals. Since the 1880s, the Fisk University Jubilee Singers and other Historically Black Colleges and University singing groups have performed spirituals, also called Jubilee songs.

Ka`a`awa

Literally meaning "the wrasse fish," it is an area on the northeast coast of the island of O`ahu.

Kamakahi, Dennis

Dennis David Kahekilimamaoikalanikeha Kamakahi (1953-2014) was a prolific composer of Hawaiian music, a famed slack-key guitarist, and a beloved Christian minister. He was nominated for numerous Grammy awards and won three times. He was inducted into the Hawaiian Music Hall of Fame in 2009. A kind and compassionate soul, he will be greatly missed. He authored and sang "Pua Hone."

Kamapua`a

The pig god in the native Hawaiian religion.

Kīlauea Volcano

The youngest volcano on the Big Island of Hawai`i. Located in Hawai`i Volcanoes National Park.

koa

Native to the Hawaiian islands, Acacia koa is a species of flowering tree in the pea family. The wood produced from it is beautiful and robust. In Hawaiian, koa means "bold, brave, and fearless" or "warrior." The tree grows at high elevations in volcanic soil with substantial rainfall. Fruit is produced after 5-30 years. Seeds can remain dormant for up to 25 years.

Ko`olau Mountains

The Windward mountain range on O`ahu.

Kwan Yin

A Buddhist Bodhisattva associated with mercy, sometimes called the Goddess of Mercy. In modern times, the name is Romanized as Guanyin.

Laoshan

A district and monastery near Qingdao, China.

Lao Tzu

Lao Tzu, aka Laozi (ca. 6th century BCE), was a Chinese philosopher and poet. His existence is legendary. He is even revered as a deity in Taoism. Scholars dispute attributions of certain works to him, for example, arguing that the Tao Te Ching was written by many individuals. The poems attributed to him have been celebrated through the ages, although clearly some of them were revised by later authors and editors.

lehua

Delicate scented flower of the `ōhi`a tree in the Hawaiian islands. Generally found in the mountains, especially on Hawai`i, the Big Island. In Hawaiian mythology, reputed to be the first tree to grow from lava.

liana

Long-stemmed, woody vines flourishing in moist, tropical environments such as rainforests and deciduous forests. They can be differentiated from trees and shrubs by their stiffness. Trees and shrubs have flexible younger growth and stiffer older growth, while lianas often manifest the reverse, with stiffer young growth and more flexible older growth.

lotus

The lotus is a type of legume and flower (sometimes called water lily) that can proliferate in a wide variety of habitats. Its taxonomy is undergoing revision. Lotuses are identified in the genus Nelumbo (Indian and American lotuses), the genus Nymphaea (blue, sacred, and star lotuses), and others. The mythological lotus tree appears in Homer's Odyssey, Ovid's Metamorphoses, and the Biblical Book of Job.

madras

A lightweight cotton fabric with patterned texture and plaid design. Its name comes from the former name of the city of Chennai, India.

Makaloa Point

An area on the North Shore of O`ahu with spectacular views.

Maui

The second-largest island in the Hawaiian islands. The other islands are Hawai`i, Kaho`olawe, Kaua`i, Lana`i, Moloka`i, Ni`ihau, and O`ahu.

Mistral

A strong, cold, northwesterly wind that blows from southern France into the northern Mediterranean.

Mokuli`i Island

Also called Chinaman's Hat. An islet near Kualoa on the island of O`ahu, named because it resembled the hats worn by Chinese plantation workers who immigrated to Hawai`i in the mid 1800s.

Moloka`i

One of the eight major islands in the Hawaiian islands. The others are Hawai`i, Kaho`olawe, Kaua`i, Lana`i, Maui, Ni`ihau, and O'ahu.

Mt. Lao

A granite mountain in Shandong Province northeast of Qingdao, it is part of Qingdao Laoshan National Park and is the highest coastal mountain in China. Traditionally affiliated with Taoism, it is considered one of the birthplaces of Taoist spiritual philosophy. The mountain is also an important historical landmark for Chinese Buddhism.

Mt. Pinatubo

An active stratovolcano in the Cabusilan Mountains on the island of Luzon in the Philippines. Assumed dormant, it erupted violently in 1991.

Mt. Tantalus

This mountain is an extinct cinder cone on the southern Ko`olau ridge above Honolūlū on the island of O'ahu. Its summit is Tantalus Crater. The site is a popular hiking and picnic spot for locals and tourists. Originally called Pu`u-ohi`a by native Hawaiians, it was renamed in modern times for the Greek god Tantalus who, always thirsty, was punished by being placed in a pool of water. When he tried to drink, the water receded. Similarly, when hikers climb, the peak appears to recede.

Nature

Nature with a capital N alludes to spirituality in everything. The word comes from the Latin natura (birth, essential qualities, innate disposition), which was translated from the Greek word physis (intrinsic characteristics of plants, animals, and the environment).

nēnē

A species of goose in the Hawaiian islands. The official bird of Hawai`i.

N'est-ce pas?

French for "Isn't it so?"

North Shore

An area on the island of O`ahu famed for water sports.

O`ahu

One of the eight major islands in the Hawaiian islands. The others are Kaho`olawe, Kaua`i, Lana`i, Maui, Moloka`i, Ni`ihau, and Hawai`i.

`ōhi`a

A hearty tree that grows out of lava once it has cooled. Its delicate and fragrant red or yellow blossoms are said to be the goddess Pele's favorite flower.

om

A symbolic mystical utterance during meditation.

Pali Lookout

A section of the windward cliffs of the Ko`olau mountains on O`ahu.

pareo

A women's one-piece wraparound garment worn in the Pacific islands.

patchouli

A bushy herb from the mint family, it is a species from the genus Pogostemon. In modern times, it is burned as incense.

Pele

The Hawaiian volcano goddess connected with the Big Island of Hawai`i and mythology.

phoenix

A bird in Greek mythology, which is cyclically regenerated or reborn out of the ashes.

pikake

A species of jasmine native to the Himalayas and India.

plumeria

A genus in the dogbane family with fragrant flowers used in lei making, also known as frangipani.

"Pua Hone"

A song written by the Hawaiian musician Dennis Kamakahi in 1977. The title literally means "honey flower," but this is not an actual flower. According to Kamakahi the term refers to "a love that's slowly nurtured in the heart."

puakenikeni

A large shrub or small tree from the South Pacific. The tiny flowers are white and fragrant, often used for lei making. It is also called the Perfume Flower Tree.

pulelehua

A type of butterfly native to the Hawaiian islands.

qigong

"Life energy cultivation," in Chinese.

Body, breath, and mind practices balancing qi (life energy).

Qingdao

A city of Shandong Province in eastern China. Located on the Yellow River, it is a major seaport and an industrial center.

Ritchie, Lionel

Lionel Brockman Ritchie, Jr. (b. 1949) is an American musician from Tuskegee, Alabama.

Roosevelt, Eleanor

Anna Eleanor Roosevelt (1884-1962) was the First Lady of the United States from 1933-1945.

Roosevelt, Franklin

Franklin Delano Roosevelt (1882-1945) was President of the United States from 1933-1945.

Rumi

Rumi, aka Jalāl ad-Dīn Muhammad Balkhī (13th century), was a Persian poet, jurist, theologian, and Sufi mystic. His works are renowned worldwide, especially his love and metaphysical poems.

Sahara

The world's hottest desert. More than 3 million square miles, it covers most of North Africa. Its name comes from the plural of the Arabic word for desert, meaning literally "deserts."

Stairway to Heaven

A popular hiking trail on O`ahu in Hawai`i. Also called Ha`ikū Stairs and Ha`ikū Ladder.

sea grape

A flowering plant in the buckwheat family native to coastal beaches in tropic areas of the Americas and the Caribbean.

Sichuan

A province in southwestern China, also called Szechwan and Setzuan, famed for its spicy cuisine, enjoyed throughout China and the world.

stela

From classical Greek and Latin, this type of stone or wooden slab is erected as a monument for funerals and commemorations. Text and decorations are carved in or painted on the slab. Confucius used such stones as teaching tablets.

Stravinsky, Igor

Igor Fyodorovich Stravinsky (1882-1971) was a Russian composer, pianist, and conductor. After Emigrating from Russia, he became a French citizen and then an American citizen.

Sugmad

In Eckankar spiritual practice, this refers to the endless source from which all forms were created.

taiji

Also called tai chi. A type of exercise and defensive marital art originating in China.

tantric

A style of meditation and ritual which arose in India no later than the 5th century AD. The concrete manifestation of the divine energy of the godhead that creates and maintains that universe, seeks to ritually appropriate and channel that energy, within the human microcosm, in creative and emancipatory ways.

ti

A woody plant in the lily family, native to tropical Asia and Australia. The leaves are put to many uses by Hawaiians from cooking to ornamental use.

21 Nocturnes

A musical composition by Frédéric François Chopin.

Tuskegee

A city in Alabama. Home to Tuskegee University, which was founded in

1881 by Booker T. Washington. Famous for training the highly decorated Tuskegee Airmen during WWII, it remains the only historically black college with a doctoral degree in Veterinary Medicine. Originally, the word Tuskegee denoted a tribal town of Creek Indians.

Volcanoes National Park

Established in 1916, Hawai`i Volcanoes National Park is located on the Big Island of Hawai`i in the Hawaiian islands, administered by the Federal Park Service of the U.S. Department of the Interior. It has two active volcanoes, Kīlauea and Mauna Loa.

Waddell, Bill

William H. Waddell IV (1908-2007) was an American Buffalo soldier, veterinarian, author, and co-founder of the Tuskegee Veterinary School.

Waddell, Lottie

Lottie Younge Waddell (1913-1989) was an American professor of English, French, and German at Tuskegee University.

Washington, Booker T.

Booker T. Washington (1856-1915) was an American author, educator, public speaker, and advisor to several U.S. presidents. Born in slavery, after the Civil War, he worked to improve the lives of African Americans through education. He founded the Tuskegee Normal School for Colored Teachers in 1881, which became the Tuskegee Institute and today is known as Tuskegee University.

"wo ai ni, cha cha chu"

Refrain from a popular Chinese song circa 2005. The phrase "wo ai ni" means "I love you." The sounds "cha cha chu" have no literal meaning.

Xian

The capital of Shaanxi Province in the central-northwest region of China.

yang

Male principle in Chinese philosophy and religion associated with sun, light, active, dominant, and hardness.

Yekaterina Alexeevna

See Catherine the Great.

Yellowstone National Park

Established in 1872, Yellowstone National Park is located primarily in the state of Wyoming but also partly in Montana and Idaho, administered by the Federal Park Service of the U.S. Department of the Interior. It is known for its wildlife and geothermal features.

yin

Female principle in Chinese philosophy and religion associated with night, dark, moon, passive, receptive, yielding, and softness.

yoga

Originating in ancient India, it consists of mental, physical, and spiritual practices. Traditions are found within Buddhism, Hinduism, and Jainism.

ABOUT THE AUTHOR

Kathryn Waddell Takara, Ph.D., is the author of six books. She is also a 2010 winner of the American Book Award (Before Columbus Foundation). She is a performance poet whose travels in Africa, Europe, Central America, Tahiti and China are often reflected in her work. She has previously published: Frank Marshall Davis: The Fire and the Phoenix (A Critical Biography) --Davis was a journalist, poet, and labor activist of the Chicago Renaissance—and Timmy Turtle Teaches, a colorful children's travel book. Her other publications include three books of poetry: from Ishmael Reed Press New and Collected Poems, and from Pacific Raven Press Pacific Raven: Hawai`i Poems, and Tourmalines: Beyond the Ebony Portal. She has also published a collection Oral Histories of African Americans in Hawai`i as well as numerous poems and scholarly articles.

Born and raised in Tuskegee, Alabama, Waddell Takara is a retired Associate Professor from the University of Hawai`i at Mānoa, where she developed courses in African American and African politics, history, literature, and culture.

Takara earned her Ph.D. in Political Science and an M.A. in French and has taught, advised, and mentored many. She has appeared on a variety of television shows and documentary films, and has given frequent interviews to publications and the media. She particularly enjoys her family and friends, pets, writing, meditation, qigong, travel, books, gardening, raising orchids and interior design.

www.kathrynwaddelltakara.com

A portion of the proceeds from the sale of this book will be donated to The United Negro College Fund. UNCF is the nation's largest and most effective minority education organization.

CPSIA information can be obtained
at www.ICGtesting.com
Printed in the USA
FSOW01n0856250914
3153FS

9 780986 075506